On being a Christian

The Hans Küng Debate

On being a Christian

The Hans Küng Debate

Leo Scheffczyk

FOUR COURTS PRESS

This book is a translation by
Fr Peadar Mac Seumais, SJ, of
*Kursänderung des Glaubens?: Theologische
Gründe zur Entscheidung im Fall Küng*
© Christiana-Verlag, CH-820 Stein am Rhein 1980,
first published in 1982 by Four Courts Press Limited,
Kill Lane, Blackrock, County Dublin, Ireland.
Printed in the Republic of Ireland.
Nihil obstat: Stephen J. Greene, censor deputatus.
Imprimi potest: Dermot Archbishop of Dublin, 8 December 1981.

ISBN 0 906127 57 2   cloth
ISBN 0 906127 58 0   paper

CONTENTS

FOREWORD

The appearance in English translation of Professor Leo Scheffczyk's critical study of the thought of Hans Küng is a more important event than the brevity of the work might lead one to expect. The not inconsiderable public which has become familiar with the writings of Küng in English translation has had, unfortunately, little access to books or articles submitting these writings to scholarly analysis and critique. Surprisingly, no book, or even pamphlet, critically appraising Küng's account of the Christian faith appears to have come from publishing firms in Ireland or Britain up to now; and even the reviews which have appeared of *On being a Christian* – the principal and best-known work in which that account is to be found – have tended to be rather general and descriptive and, in many instances, have surprisingly failed to signal its radical defects. Also, much attention has been devoted to the procedures whereby Küng was deprived by the Holy See of the right to teach in the name of the Catholic Church, to the neglect of the primary issues concerning the orthodoxy of his doctrine and the validity, from a Catholic standpoint, of his basic theological method.

For these reasons, and because of the intrinsic merits of the work itself, this English translation of Professor Scheffczyk's incisive study deserves to be widely read. Scheffczyk, who teaches dogmatic theology at Munich University, and was formerly a colleague of Küng's in Tübingen, is, regrettably, not very well known in the English-speaking world. No one reading the pages of this book, however, will be left in any doubt about his wide and deep scholarship and his singularly penetrating intelligence. These qualities, together with lucidity of style and complete scholarly integrity, are the characteristic marks of his writings. In addition to innumerable articles, these include a dozen or more substantial books covering a wide range of theological topics. Scheffczyk is also pre-eminently 'a man of the Church', who has made a deep study of the development of Christian doctrine over the centuries and who makes no apologies for his complete fidelity to the Church's teaching. How effectively theological work on this basis can make contact with the concerns of modern thought and culture can be readily seen from a perusal of his writings.

Scheffczyk's critique of Küng is cogently argued and penetrates to the very core of his thought. A point to which the book repeatedly returns is that Küng's writings do not stand up to critical examination by his peers. Unfortunately, however, they can impress those who are not expert in theology. Küng often accuses his critics — the Roman Curia, the German bishops, theologians who disagree with him — of ignorance and lack of scholarship. Scheffczyk here shows convincingly that the boot is on the other foot. The same is true of the charge of stubbornness, of unwillingness or incapacity to learn from criticism, which Küng frequently makes against his opponents.

No doubt Scheffczyk's devastating criticism will come as a surprise to some. They will scarcely be prepared for a study which so clearly shows the depth and range of Küng's sad betrayal of traditional Catholic teaching. That Küng has rejected the Catholic teaching on infallibility has for some time now been fairly widely known. It was principally his refusal to withdraw from this position that led, in December 1979, to his being deprived of his licence to teach in the name of the Catholic Church. But it is no doubt possible that someone who does not accept the doctrine of infallibility may still, by and large, retain intact the central truths of divine revelation. Many people will be under the impression that this is true of Hans Küng. They do not see any reason, therefore, why they should not take him at his word when he undertakes to present Christian teaching on God, salvation, the Church etc., in a way newly relevant to modern life and better adapted to the demands of the contemporary critical intelligence.

Readers of this work of Scheffczyk will scarcely take this view. For Scheffczyk shows quite clearly that Küng's denial of the infallible magisterium of the Church was no isolated abberation, but the prelude to a rejection of the Church's teaching on a whole range of issues, many of them central to the Christian Gospel.

That is not to say that Küng's books *On being a Christian* and *Does God exist?* are without merit. They do contain a great deal that is useful and stimulating, but this is linked to interpretations of Church teaching which to a large extent empty Christian faith of its real substance. Küng indeed set out with a very laudable aim. He wished to make the faith of the Church more accessible to the contemporary mind. In certain ways he succeeds in doing that, but unfortunately only at the price of a radical reduction of its content. Küng's version of Christianity has certainly impressed many readers as plausible and attractive, but it is precisely this which betrays its fatal flaw: in order to make the Gospel reasonable and credible in the eyes of the modern world he has removed from it much that that world finds most difficult to accept.

As Professor Joseph Ratzinger (now Cardinal Archbishop of Munich) pointed out a few years ago, this procedure might still have been defensible if Küng had declared that he was merely presenting those elements of the Gospel which unbelievers or marginal Christians could most easily

9

understand and accept. If he had been content to label his *On being a Christian* simply a *summa pro paganis*, he would have let it be seen that there was still much to be added, that what the book contained would need to be amplified, deepened, even re-stated or corrected. However, by expressly presenting it as sufficient to meet all the essential needs of the Christian believer, by insisting that it be considered a veritable *summa pro Christianis*, he sacrificed his right to be regarded henceforth as an authentic witness to the Gospel of Christ in its integrity.

At the end of this volume the reader will find Statements on the Küng affair from the Roman Congregation for the Doctrine of the Faith and the German Episcopal Conference. They are important for any objective assessment of the question as to whether Küng was fairly treated. The Declaration of the German Bishops in particular testifies to the many efforts that were made to bring the controversy concerning Küng's writings to a conclusion acceptable to all concerned.

I wish this little volume a wide readership. Its significance is not confined to the case of Hans Küng and his writings. It is also relevant to opinions similar to his which are being put forward by other prominent theologians writing today. Coming as it does from a theologian of the first rank whose own considerable contribution to theology and theological renewal is beyond question, it cannot be suspected of lack of sympathy for the theologian's task. On the contrary, its severe criticism reflects its author's concern for the integrity of that task and his painful awareness of the bitter fruits a misguided theology can bring.

+ KEVIN McNAMARA

INTRODUCTION

This essay was commissioned by my publisher, who had received many requests for a theological assessment of Hans Küng's writings. Such an assessment seems opportune in view of the Holy See's decision of December 1979, which led to the withdrawal of Küng's licence to teach in the Catholic theology faculty of the University of Tübingen.

Nowadays the danger that the faith may become contaminated[1] should not be lightly dismissed. With the opening of the Church to the world — an opening which everyone supports and whose positive aspects must not be criticised — all the negative features of the secular world are also found to be surfacing. These are: opportunism; attempts to adapt to and to court the majority; and all the herd phenomena which Ortega y Gasset foresaw in the thirties as the fate of the coming age (it would be, he said, swept on by every new current, fascinated by freedom from control, despising tradition and adopting a frivolous approach to everything).[2]

The question may nevertheless be asked: Is examination of Hans Küng's teachings appropriate at this time? Before the Roman decree was issued, it was said that the influence of Küng's theology was on the wane (apart from reverberations in the media), and that what needed more attention today was 'liberation theology', rather than this late fruit of theological liberalism. Indeed, many advocates of 'liberation theology' have dismissed Küng, pointing to his 'appallingly reactionary political position, and lack of sensitivity.'[3] Should attention therefore not be directed to other matters more important than an out of date, western theological phenomenon?

Yet it is a fact that Hans Küng has deeply penetrated and almost saturated the intellectual atmosphere of our time. His writings have long ceased to be merely isolated events. They have met a ready welcome from the spirit of the age, which has given them a considerable resonance and used them to express resentments, conscious dislikes, and unconscious yearnings for a Christianity that would not merely be renewed but would be born again from the womb of our time as something completely new. These growing tendencies are noticeable in Küng's recent book *Existiert Gott?* referred to in this book as DG (English title: *Does God exist?*). In it there is a constant call for a 'change of course'. This does not mean some mild 'cosmetic' changes but, quite bluntly, an essential change of Christianity, carried out in the spirit of a popularised version of post-Hegelian philosophy.[4] Such tendencies as these cannot be let go uncontradicted.

It is also objected that controversies about the faith always do harm. What is needed today, above all, is the showing forth of Christian love. Only that can convince the world – not dogmatic statements of 'theoretical' truths. In fact some of the success of Küng's books is due not least to his absolute avoidance of unambiguous confession of the faith of the Church, and of dogma (which he treats as a later invention of unchristian hellenism).

The answer to this objection is that the separation of truth from love is a sophistry which leads ultimately to an error to which the average Christian conscience is easily exposed. For, love of truth is an essential aspect of love; without a basic love of truth, a person cannot have true love. It is the effort to find the truth which reveals to man the vision of the lovable in the world, and particularly, in people. Thus a love without truth would become a sentimental feeling of happiness (just as truth without love can admittedly degenerate into rigidity of outlook). But these two basic attitudes to life are essentially inseparable: love requires that a person should not withhold from his neighbour the testimony to the truth. As Dietrich Bonhoeffer said: 'It is only when a man does not withhold the truth from another man that he is acting towards him like a brother. If I do not tell him the truth, then I am treating him as a heathen. If I speak the truth to one who has a different opinion, that is an act of the love which I owe to him'.[5]

Bearing witness to the truth calls for real intellectual effort and struggle. Among Christians today there is probably no one who would doubt that Jesus Christ brought to mankind the Gospel of love and confirmed it with an unique proof of love. But should one exclude from the original core of the Gospel that element which determines its character as a message of victory? (Nowadays the Gospel is often inadequately defined as 'Good News' placed at the disposition of each individual.) Yet the promulgation and transmission of a victory message necessitate controversy and intellectual struggle. The whole life of Jesus was marked by such a struggle for the truth, without that resulting in a diminution of his love for men. Even the early Christian community was also subject to this requirement: St Paul reminded them that someone might come 'and preach another Christ whom we do not preach, or that you may receive another Spirit whom you have not received' (2 Cor 11:4). They too, early on, had to learn a lesson which we still find difficult to understand – that the greatest dangers to the faith come from within (cf. Act 20:30) and that therefore they must 'fight the good fight, in the secure possession of the faith and of a good conscience' (1 Tim 1:19).

To appeal to a good conscience is a bold claim. Nevertheless, those may lay claim to it who did not begin this present controversy, who did not seek strife, but who, out of reverence for the unassailable truth of Jesus

Christ, are concerned to preserve it pure and inviolate. They cannot and therefore do not wish to deny the good faith of their opponents, but neither can they help feeling that there is on the other side a growing hardening towards the Church, a more irreconcilable attitude, a greater shrillness of tone. The author of *Christ sein** (referred to in this book as Chr; English title: *On being a Christian*) and *Does God exist?* published an article devoted to a critical assessment of the person and achievement of the Pope, on the occasion of the first anniversary of his election. This article, modestly entitled 'An Enquiry', written in a style full of neat phrases, attacked the Pope's personal character, calling him 'a superstar', 'a doctrinaire defender of old defensive positions', 'a dictator'; it attacked him also as being theologically uninformed, as being engaged in inquisitorial procedures, and accused him of neglecting human rights in the Church. These expressions are hardly to be measured by normal standards.[6] The criticism goes to the length of asking: 'Can one imagine Jesus of Nazareth like this?', and: is this 'a real Christian?' It is also clear that Küng is putting forward a fundamentally new principle of Church leadership and teaching, a principle which dramatically expresses the 'change of course' he keeps calling for in *Does God exist?* At the beginning of this article Küng refers to an international group of theologians and the document published by them at the time of the papal election – 'The pope we need'. This document he takes as the norm by which the pope, his Christian character, and Chriatianity in general are to be measured, if the Church is to become what it is supposed to be. This claim is not just exaggerated: it is founded on an absolute subjective certainty of personal possession of the truth. This is clear from the concluding appeal to the authority of Pope Gregory the Great, who declared that a dispute about what is the truth must be tolerated rather than that the truth itself be abandoned. This final remark can only mean that Küng claims a few theologians (or only one) hold the truth – and the Church does not.

Here is a 'change of course', a course correction, which could hardly be more radical. Anyone who wants to avoid being swept away by this irrational current, or who wants to preserve his intellectual freedom to control this change of course, must examine the entire direction Küng is sailing in. In fact he can't help asking: Is this ship not being steered towards a mark fastened to its own bowsprit?

The following pages are not intended to be polemical. They are not written in a desire for conflict, or for a victory over someone who thinks or believes differently. It is not my aim to make a list of errors and mistakes, but rather to learn from the mistakes, and to clarify the truth against the background of error. Genuine theology has always seen this as its objective in the controversies it had to engage in. This was how Origen (+ *c.*

254) put it: 'Contradiction lays siege to Catholic doctrine, so that our faith may not grow stiff in repose, but may be exercised and become pure. For this reason the Apostle said "Heresies must come, so that those things which are approved may become manifest", and so that the truth "may shine as silver purified in the fire"'. Johann Möhler (+ 1838), one of the leaders of the Catholic Tübingen school, quoting Origen, added: 'The truth is developed and becomes bright through intellectual struggle. . . . It leaves the error to others, and retains for itself the truth which develops from the error; and this no one will grudge it'.[7]

I

THE OUTCOME
OF THE DEBATE ABOUT
ON BEING A CHRISTIAN
OR, THE RISE
OF A NEW INSTITUTION

Christ sein is admittedly written in an earnest, spirited and gripping style. It raised a great storm in part of the ecclesiastical world, and among theological scholars it started a controversy in which many took part.[8]

On reviewing this theological debate, one comes to the conclusion that the verdict of the professional theologians was distinctly critical and negative: this was in contrast to the enthusiasm of the non-theological public. The theologians conceded Küng's positive pastoral concern and expressed their criticism in conciliatory terms, for the most part. This was a pleasant change from the journalistic polemic preferred by Küng. Adhering to a systematic plan, they sought to indicate the erroneous statements in the book, criticising them from the standpoint of the Catholic faith, and to clarify and deepen this standpoint. In German-speaking countries special mention must be made of a collection of essays entitled *Diskussion über H. Küngs 'Christ sein'*[9], ... which analyses Küng's more important errors in dogma, history of dogma and biblical theology. J. Ratzinger, writing on 'Method' points out that Küng's 'theology is consistently developed without reference to dogma, and even against dogma'.[10] 'It is characteristic of Küng that in his book about infallibility he holds the principle that a dogma is not a permanently binding declaration'.[11] W. Kasper goes in the same direction; he points out that a fundamental principle of theology is missing — the unity of Scripture, Tradition and Magisterium: 'These three form together an indissoluble unity: for the actual Scripture and Tradition are to be found only in the Church, in the actual Church which is in communion with the Apostolic See'.[12] A favourite argument of Küng for the relativisation of the truth about Christ is based on the history of dogma and makes use of the 'Hellenisation hypothesis'[13] long since abandoned by historical science. This is examined in depth by A. Grillmeier, who comes to the conclusion: 'It is quite clear that the Council of

15

Nicea did not amount to a hellenisation of Christianity, but a rejection of hellenisation, a liberation of the Christian concept of God from the narrowing and splitting tendency of hellenism. The Greek philosophers did not conquer Nicea: Nicea conquered the Greeks'.[14] Here also it is noticeable that Küng has not kept abreast of modern research into the history of philosophy and theology. His assertions about hellenisation coincide with ideas already put forward in the seventeenth century − for example by the Protestant dogmatic theologian N. Souverain (+ 1700).[15]

The exegete J. Kremer takes up a particular theological question − the way the book depicts Jesus. Referring to the evangelical theologians F. Hohn and Albert Schweitzer, he points out that 'once the historical Jesus is separated from the rock of the teaching of the Church, the interpreter falls under the influence of the outlook of his own time'.[16] The trinitarian doctrine of the book raises, according to the dogmatic theologian T. Schneider, the question whether a reader wishing to discover the essence of Christianity would not gain the impression 'firstly that the doctrine of the Trinity is of no great importance in the whole structure of Christianity; secondly, that in the past, spectacular efforts in this area have borne little fruit, and have contributed little to a genuine understanding of God; and thirdly, that the significance of Jesus Christ for us and our Christianity is to be explained without reference to all this'.[17]

More decisively Hans Urs von Balthasar takes up a point which is central in the Christian doctrine of redemption. It is a good example of how easily the assertions of *On being a Christian* change colour and can deceive the unsuspecting reader. The case in point is the simple sentence 'Als der zum Leben bei Gott Erweckte ist und bleibt Jesus für uns (ein für allemal) der Gekreuzigte' [which Quinn translates as: 'As the one raised to life with God, he is and remains the crucified for us (once and for all)']. Von Balthasar points out that this sentence is not 'truly Christian'.[18] For it to be Christian it is not enough to acknowledge that 'Jesus is for us the one who was crucified'. The interpretation of the cross of Christ is truly Christian only when it is acknowledged that 'Jesus is the one who was crucified for us'. The tiny change in the position of the words 'for us' opens up a great gap in the understanding of Christ's nature. The statement 'Jesus is and remains for us the crucified one' means something essentially different from saying that he 'is the one who was crucified for us'. The first statement expresses, as something purely extrinsic, the fact that Jesus died on the cross, and that we can recognise this death as an exemplary event, a prototype or example. Thus a purely extrinsic, perhaps even ethical, relationship of men to the death of Jesus is established. This is, however, far from the true doctrine that Jesus died for us and as our intrinsic and essential representative has freed us from sin. In fact, the concept of a vicarious atonement and real deliverance of sinners through the crucifixion is not expressed until one declares unambiguously that 'Jesus is the one who was crucified for us', i.e. that he died for us. The 'for us' must continue to be recognised as an intrinsic and essential element of the death of Jesus Christ. It must not merely indicate a vague kind of additional importance attaching to the death of Jesus. In the first case, the faith recognises a profound and essential effect produced in mankind by the cross of Christ; in the other there is a statement of the fact as something purely extrinsic. This statement could well have come from the Pelagians of old: they did not believe in the intrinsic redemptive efficacy of the death of Christ, but only in its power to influence by example. At any rate the vicarious atoning and redemptive death of Jesus Christ is not expressed in the sentence referred to. The source of this defect in Küng is to be found at a deeper level: in his interpretation of Christ, since only a God-man would be able to free mankind from its sins, and the death of a mere 'advocate, spokesman, counsel or friend' of God (such are the many descriptions given by Küng) cannot in fact clear away the sins of mankind.

Of course, it may be asked if *On being a Christian*, with its ill-defined concepts and wall-poster language, is at all capable of using such a distinction. Yet, to neglect this distinction is ultimately disastrous for the Catholic faith. Another discrepancy, this time in Marian doctrine, is just as disastrous. H. Riedlinger says that the view of Mary presented in the book shows 'a concept appropriate to the radical rationalism of the Enlightenment' which avoids 'any appearance of identification with the official dogmatic declarations of the Catholic Church'.[19] As a result, the book never mentions 'belief about Mary', and Küng's 'programme of radical rationalism demands a withdrawal in the area of Marian doctrine'. Such an easy-going 'withdrawal' would be 'the road to ruin for the Church'.[20]

K. Lehmann points out that the route Küng takes would not even serve the ecumenical concern strongly expressed in the book. By avoiding the christological and trinitarian teaching of the early councils he undermines the doctrinal consensus which has already been attained with the Orthodox and with many churches of the Reform. Lehmann's final and unambiguous conclusion is similar: the book merely guides its reader into 'ecclesial homelessness' and strengthens the tendency towards a 'third confession of faith'.[21]

A similar fear is expressed by Karl Rahner in his examination of the ecclesiology put forward in this book. He points out that 'the leaders in the Church would consequently be mere functionaries whom the mass of Christians, all equal in rights, give to themselves'.[22] He also rightly doubts whether the Christian imperatives and demands contained in the book are really inseparably connected with the person of Jesus Christ and are not in fact the expression of an idealised humanism. This is confirmed by B. Stoeckle also, writing from the standpoint of Christian ethics. He sees in Küng's 'autonomous morality' the operation of an autonomous rationality which is merely human, and which does not result in the following of Christ but only produces 'a superficial display of those characteristics of Jesus which fit in with the modern pleasure-orientated life-style'.[23] In fact, the attitudes Küng recommends, such as maturity, acceptance of the world, intellectual honesty, have nothing specifically Christian about them. The Christian attitude can only be derived from the absolute value of holiness. Another author, referring to the new Christian morality emphatically recommended in this book, has spoken of a 'banalisation of Christianity'[24], which turns out to be so colourless and unoriginal that one could ask what being a Christian adds to being just a human being.

H. Küng's answer to the book containing these various criticisms is, in its tone, style and content, characteristic of the level of debate he has introduced. The eleven theologians are first reminded that they have taken the field with 'the strength of a football team; once more, eleven against one'; they are in fact 'supported by an imposing number of zealous flag-wavers, and by the trumpets of archconservative Catholic popular press.'[25] It is already clear that he is not interested in dialogue, or even in debate. Against the serious criticism of the lack of harmony of his theology with the teaching of the Church, his only answer is 'No: there will be no discussion here on such a level'.

Even in the body of his statement he doesn't really answer the questions raised. Instead he refers ironically to the lack of unity in this 'team'; he reproaches them with alleged false compromises with orthodoxy, with mysticism, with a harmonising history of dogma, and accuses them of not thinking progressively: they constantly cry 'Halt' and do not point to any way forward.

This style of controversy, which proceeds on the principle that attack is the best form of defence, is not without its effect on the spectator — particularly the non-theologian. However, it doesn't help to clarify the issues. In view of such a total refusal to consider the objections, even the non-theologian must ask himself whether so many theologians can be so wrong that they entirely misunderstand an author, and misread his well-intentioned propositions. And another question must be asked: How do the examination of conscience and readiness to change which Küng constantly calls for, fit in with his own absolute stubbornness and self-confidence — especially since his position cannot rely upon, and even rejects any legitimation by, tradition and the teaching of the Church.

Sometimes he dismisses this kind of controversy as mere theological wrangling. He is obviously trying to diminish the weight of these objections and to accentuate what he claims to be the sparkling vitality and closeness to real life of his new brand of Christianity. But it must be pointed out that many who are not specialist theologians have taken part in the debate – teachers of religious knowledge, ministers of religion, pastoral workers. They rightly sense that it is not merely about esoteric scholarly problems, but about the very foundations of Christian and Catholic faith and life.

One impressive example of a line of thought deriving from a genuine instinct of faith, without any use of theological concepts or systematical framework, is given by E. Laws in his reply to Küng.[26] It is not necessary to dwell upon Laws' – valid – comments on the style and method of argument used in *On being a Christian*: the 'fog-words'; 'jellyfish concepts'; 'caricatures'; 'foxhole tactics' by which in each sentence a subordinate clause is kept open, apparently leading in another direction. But emphasis must be laid on Laws' basic judgment about the essential Christianity which Küng describes in his book and offers as the final victory over the wretched condition of the Christian churches. According to Laws, the book has two different attitudes to the understanding of Scripture: if one accepts Scripture as 'a message inspired by the Spirit and as a book of the Church, one cannot write off essential parts such as the nucleus of St John's Gospel as later interpretations made by the Church'. His judgment is equally clear about the important special question of the personality of the Holy Spirit. On this question the author of *On being a Christian*, after distorting many declarations of the Church, comes to the following conclusion: 'He [the Holy Spirit] is God himself in so far as he, as a merciful power and strength, wins control over the interior, the heart of man, indeed over the whole of man, and is interiorly present to man, and gives effective testimony of himself to man's spirit'. Laws rightly sums up this conception: 'So what we call the Holy Spirit is nothing other than God's merciful action upon us men'.[27] Laws' judgment about the book's trinitarian doctrine is equally to the point. According to *On being a Christian* this doctrine is more an explanation of a dynamic action of God in history and more about his relation to mankind, than about the mystery of God's own life. Thus the conclusion of Laws is consistent: 'The doctrine about Jesus Christ is inseparable from the doctrine of the Trinity. If there is a triune God, then Jesus can and must be the incarnate Son of God, in the proper sense of these words. But if there is no real Trinity, then Jesus cannot at any time be really the Son of God'.[28] Laws says that the alleged roots of this 'Christianity', in a Jesus of Nazareth who is so highly praised in words, are up in the air: since 'Küng's basic dogma (he calls it a "thesis") is that the decisive feature of Christianity is Christ Jesus himself, and this is only a fragment of the truth.'[29] From this criticism it becomes clear that *On being a Christian* offers only a crumbling fragment of a disintegrating Christianity.

In the course of the debate it has become obvious that the kind of Christianity recommended by the Tübingen theologian has raised strong opposition. This opposition does not arise, as he suggests, because his critics are followers of the ancient Greek mode of thought, or are antiquated 'neo-Scholastics' (among them are reckoned H. Urs von Balthasar, A. Grillmeier[30] and Michael Schmaus[31]; and the term 'neo-scholasticism' is not explained even in outline). The distinction between those writers and Küng is not between 'old' and 'new', 'antiquated' and 'modern', 'traditional' and 'progressive'; it is much more a matter of two different kinds of faith or (if I may say so) of two Christianities.

The magisterium's decision to investigate Küng's doctrinal views shows that this controversy is about more than mere emphases or clarifications of the Christian faith. After the disagreement (which appeared also in the *The Church* and *Infallible?*) had seemed to have been removed by a really generous statement by the Congregation for the Doctrine of the Faith[32], the German episcopal conference found it necessary to issue a statement soon after the appearance of *On being a Christian*.[33] In this statement they acknowledged the theological effort and pastoral objectives of the book in most conciliatory terms, but they did criticise a series of assertions (especially about Christology, the doctrine of the Trinity, the theology of the Church and the sacraments, as well as the role of Mary in the history of salvation); the bishops could not see how these assertions could be reconciled, as they should be, with the interpretation of these truths transmitted by the tradition of the Church.[34]

Soon after this the German bishops issued a statement 'About the Nicene profession of faith concerning Christ'. Without mentioning any names, they spoke of their concern 'that, in theological discussions, interpretations of Christology had emerged which did not seem reconcilable with the faith of the Church'.[35]

But Hans Küng insisted that he 'has never intended to cast doubt on the divine sonship of Jesus, or on the Trinity'.[36] An attempt was consequently made to hold a conversation between him and the representatives of the hierarchy, together with some specialist theologians, with a view to clarifying the controversial theses.

It is difficult to give an adequate account of a conversation of this kind.[37] It is possible, nevertheless, to describe fairly accurately its general tenour and the central question involved. The real and only concern of the bishops present was to obtain a positive answer to the question: 'Is Jesus Christ the Son of God, in the sense of the early councils, truly and really?' (The technical expression is 'ontologically').[38] After Küng's previous assertion that the divine sonship of Jesus could not be doubted, one would have expected a positive answer. Instead, Küng limited himself to saying that 'God himself is near to us in Jesus; was at work, spoke, acted and made a definitive revelation of himself in Jesus'.[39] His concluding statement was: 'How the divine sonship is to be interpreted afresh: that is indeed a question, is it not?'[40] This shows clearly that he had given no answer to the question about the divine sonship of Jesus. He kept insisting that the divine sonship of Christ must be interpreted, just as one has to interpret the incarnation. He spontaneously emphasised that 'in these questions he had made no definite decision'.[41] Thus, without wanting to do so, he showed the weakness of his theological position.

It is a basic Catholic principle that the meaning of a dogma remains fixed.[42] If this were not so, then, for example, the regular confession of faith in Christ which is contained in the Creed of the Church, would have no definite meaning. Of course, a theologian knows that every dogma can and must be *theologically* interpreted. But he also knows that the interpretation cannot produce a meaning other than the meaning which the dogma expresses. The work of interpretation as such is never finished and will always advance; but for this very reason, one must say that what is to be believed is not the interpretation, but the meaning itself; and this meaning must also shine out from every correct and right interpretation.

Since Küng was not able, in this conversation with the bishops, to affirm belief in the truly divine sonship of Jesus Christ, but only held firmly to the interpretation that 'God is acting in Christ', they tried to persuade him to add to his controversial statements some short supplementary declarations or corrections, and to do this within an appropriate time. To this he replied that the problems raised were not his exclusively but must be the concern of all theologians. He declared that for physical reasons he personally was not in a position to make definite supplementary declarations or corrections of this kind within a foreseeable time, and said that his next book, soon to be published, would try 'to say something of what I am also saying here, in order to clear up some other difficulties, circumstances permitting'.[43] Anyone who heard this reply could have seen in it a promising concession. A closer analysis, however, would have shown, even at the time, that the main statement was already deprived of its significance by the addition of the words 'of what I am also saying here'.

After the failure of the conversation the bishops again requested some clarifying statements about the controverted theses. They put three precise questions to him: (1) 'Is Jesus Christ the uncreated eternal Son of God consubstantial with the Father?'; (2) 'Do you agree . . . finally without reservation with the Creed of the Church that Jesus Christ is truly God and truly man?'; (3) 'Is the Creed of the Church (for example about the divine sonship of Jesus) the premise that the theologian has to interpret with all possible methods available to him?'[44] These questions received no answer. Instead came once more a reference to the fact 'that the whole problem concerning the question of God and of the basis of faith and knowledge would be given profound consideration and set down in a book of almost nine hundred pages'.[45] In a later letter he described it as 'unreasonable to demand from me, an university professor of Catholic theology, a confession of faith – as if I had ever denied it'.[46]

Next, the German episcopal conference issued a statement about *On being a Christian*, in the course of which it said: 'The method followed by Professor Küng – if logically followed through – would result in a break with the Catholic tradition of belief and teaching. The pursuit of theology without accepting the traditional faith of the Church, and the capricious selection of portions of Holy Scripture, lead to a diminution of the content of the faith'.[47] Professor Küng 'does not propose to the reader the whole Christ and his saving action in all its fulness. It is not enough to affirm in general terms one's loyalty to the indispensable articles of faith: these must, rather, be unambiguously expressed and their content must be developed'.[48]

Küng then published a statement in the press. He asked: 'When will the bishops finally allow me to work in peace?'. He added that the bishops were 'failing in patience and understanding'; he accused them of doctrinaire self-justification . . . without self-criticism'; and asserted that modern men do not expect condemnations from their pastors, but 'constructive answers to questions which are also questions for them'.[49]

At the end of this phase of the controversy came an 'appeal for understanding', and this from an author who attacked the bishops' declaration for its 'half-truths, twisting the truth, misinterpretations, misunderstandings, and even untruths'.[50] He spoke of an 'intractable magisterium'[51], of 'inquisitorial methods',[52] and warned the bishops 'not to try to play the theologian'.[53] Basically this amounts to denying the bishops the right to influence the teaching of the Church and is an express limitation of their role to that of 'Church leadership'[54], a function which Küng does not define.

The way Küng pushed back the limits of the authority of the magisterium shows that in the whole discussion there was more at issue than a controversy about some articles of faith (which certainly would have been important enough). For it became increasingly clear that he wanted to change the organisation of the Church. According to him the magisterium should no longer use theologians merely as advisers; nor should it venture to intervene in doctrinal matters: the theologian claims the right to define how, in the situation of the moment, doctrine is to be interpreted, and to decide what the Church may do and permit for the fulfilment of its task.

To justify this shift in the balance of authority in the Church, Küng appeals not only to his own authority as a theologian and that of some colleagues, but also (as if the Church were an institution subject to referenda) to the many Christians who have declared that they agree with his teaching.[55] He had already spoken of the possibility of publishing a dossier containing reviews of all the comments in praise of *On being a Christian*. This dossier would testify to the *sensus fidelium* prevailing in the Church today and at the same time show the 'hopes of great sections of our people'.[56] Now it is true that the *sensus fidelium* is an important and valid source of knowledge of the true faith, but yet never independently of the magisterium of the bishops. Because he ignores this essential element he shows that he considers it legitimate to appeal to a court of believers (and of their leaders, theologians) *against* the episcopate.

This approach has been in fact promoted in some circles. One reputable Catholic magazine, addressing itself to those who cannot identify with Küng, wrote: 'Hans Küng, through the growing popularity of his books, has become something of an "institution", not without power and influence', which represents 'a kind of authority'.[57] Indeed, an Irish journalist, T. P. O'Mahony, earlier than this, had put it even more clearly: 'But in the meantime Küng himself is a sort of phenomenon or even an "institution" with which Rome must learn to live. Whether this is good or bad, the old days, when the Vatican had the last word, are gone, perhaps for ever'.[58]

These statements come not from detractors of Küng: they are inferred from the facts by his friends, who know the real situation. Thus there is agreement on all sides on this point. This compels one to acknowledge that, in this controversy, structural intellectual movements have occurred, which have raised up a new institution inside the institution of the Church.

DOES GOD EXIST?:
COMPOUNDING AN ERROR

In spite of the rigid position he occupied at the end of the controversy about *On being a Christian*, many people still hoped that Küng would keep his promise to clear up any misunderstandings which remained. In the discussion with the bishops, he had certainly given the assurance: 'I should like to say just this much, that what I have written is not the full answer [to the Christological question] : the possibility of completion . . . this I strongly affirm. I think that I myself will be able to say more when I get down to considering this matter once again, and this I will certainly do, sooner or later. . . . With each book, I have learned so much more that I hope I will not remain standing still in the future'.[59] He promised therefore that *Does God exist?* would give the full answer; and in fact, in its opening pages, the relation of this to *On being a Christian* is so described: 'The two books are mutually complementary and – we hope – merge smoothly one into the other' (DG xxiii).

What are we to make of this completion? The judgment I offer in the following pages does not at first deal with all the points one by one. It begins with a general description and criticism of his essential line of argument. This is no easy task: Küng develops his argument with so much biographical detail, so many anecdotes and stories, that it is difficult to follow him. At the end of each long section, a conclusion, succinctly expressed and distinctively printed, is proposed to the reader. But a critical reader will notice that often the conclusion does not follow from what has gone before, and that the logical nexus is conclusive only in the subjective opinion of the author.

In general this long book, which has many good literary qualities, is designed as an answer to the modern problem of God's existence. The answer is entirely positive, and comes right at the beginning: 'Yes, God exists. And as human beings in the twentieth century we certainly can reasonably believe in God, even in the Christian God' (DG *xxiii*). Küng feels that this answer has never been properly justified in the past, since it was based on the extreme of rationalism or on the opposite extreme of an unreasoning irrational faith. This is demonstrated in Section A, particularly by contrasting Descartes and Pascal. Moreover, Küng says that until now there was no correct understanding of God, since he was seen as a static, unchangable being separate from the world.

'The new understanding of God' (Section B), which is his objective, begins to make its appearance in Hegel, but is subject to the 'The challenge of atheism' (Section C) and nihilism (Section D); 'yes to reality' is proposed as an alternative to nihilism (Section E) and 'yes to God' as an alternative to atheism (Section F); next comes Section G: 'Yes to the Christian God'. The book seeks in this way to make full use of all the answers offered to the question about God's existence in the entire intellectual history of the West, but it does this according to the over-restrictive model of the 'two possibilities'.

This model takes account of rationalistic and irrational approaches to God; in practice it ignores the third approach, that of the so-called 'trans-cendental' demonstration of God's existence, which follows from the interior dynamism of the human spirit (Fichte, Maréchal, Blondel).

After this unusual approach, Küng gives his own answer to the question of how the existence of God is to be demonstrated. He would like to occupy a central position, between a rationalistic proof from reason, and an irrational faith. It should, he says, be an 'enlightened', a 'radically rational' faith in God, but should not be grounded on reason in the sense of Vatican I (that is, grounded on the proofs of God's existence). This would be, he says, rationalism once again. Nevertheless, reason must not be excluded: this faith, while not being rationalistic, should be rational (the difference between these two concepts is not obvious). Thus, he asserts that belief in God is not the result of an 'argument from reason', but comes from a 'trust in reason' (DG 439). This trust is based on reality itself: 'The affirm-ation of God also rests, in the last resort, on a *decision*, which, again, is con-nected with the fundamental decision for reality as a whole' (DG 569). But since this confidence must not be established by preceding rational argu-ments, it must become clearly correct and convincing *while it is being pro-duced* – in its practice and from experience. Here the question immediately suggests itself: Who is to show that this experience is a valid experience?: to do this is impossible without a judgment of reason about the experience in question.

It is with this new formula that Küng hopes to encounter both modern atheism and nihilism. He does not seek to give a strictly rational and reasoned refutation of these great adversaries of belief in God. Such a theological attempt would be of course, in his opinion, rationalism again, or a rationalistic demonstration of the superiority of belief over non-belief: 'atheism cannot be eliminated rationally. It is irrefutable. . . . The denial of God cannot be refuted purely rationally' (DG 569).

The same holds true for 'nihilism'. (Nihilism is nowhere exactly defined.) In one place he says that nihilism is the groundless acceptance of an intrinsic contradiction in existential reality (cf. DG 566f), while in another place this intrinsic contradiction is considered to be an essential component of reality – from which it would follow that nihilism is true. But belief in God is in the same position (as atheism and nihilism); it can neither be established by reason, nor be refuted by reason: in this way Küng steers himself into a situation of checkmate: all the possible solutions (atheism, nihilism, belief in God) are equally acceptable and unacceptable.

Nihilism cannot be refuted by reason although it is also said to be unprovable (DG 423, 424). The consequent danger – that all three systems are equally possible, and their conclusions equally valid – becomes all the greater when Küng grants to atheists (whom he excuses as people who have opted for the spirit of the age without full reflection) that they also say yes to reality. But it is ultimately 'a basic confidence without a basis' (DG 569). 'It is a paradoxical fundamental confidence' (ibid.). The fundamental confidence must be founded on nothing other than belief in God, although the believer in God must recognise that the world is unfulfilled and in strife. But in the bold venture and risk of faith, man experiences the ultimate foundation of reality and with it at the same time the 'radical reasonableness of reason'. Yet earlier on Küng repeatedly said that reason is not certain of itself and cannot be the foundation of belief in God.

Thus the question arises here too: Is this explanation of the radical reasonableness of faith proved, or is it simply a playing with words? Either way it certainly contradicts the teaching of the Church on the natural knowledge of God, as defined in Vatican I (DS 3004, 3026). The teaching of that Council Küng expressly rejects as 'a superficial juxtaposition of reason and faith' (DG 5135). He also accuses it of splitting the idea of one God into a 'natural' and a 'supernatural' God (DG 516). This reproach shows that Küng makes no distinction in the book between natural knowledge of God and belief in the God of mystery, of supernatural love and salvation.

At this point he seems inclined to adopt an idea of God which is purely natural and philosophical; and this is confirmed by later remarks. The concept of God which man acquires through the 'fundamental confidence' (which does not differ essentially from confidence in God) he constructs principally in connection with the philosophy of Hegel. Thus, one must assert 'a correlation between God and man, between divine and human reason' (DG 183). 'Divine reason and human reason are not to be separated', even though 'they are not identical' (DG 183). The new understanding of God is therefore contained in the formula 'God is in this world and this world is in God' (DG 185), a definition which theologians previously called 'panentheism'. By this is meant the idea that God, while not identical with the world, is thought of as being necessarily bound up with it and unable to exist without it. This is enunciated in Küng's remark: 'God is oriented to the world: there is not a God without the world' (DG 672). With such a panentheistic belief in God, belief in the Trinity (and consequently belief in the true divine sonship of Jesus Christ) cannot survive. This is shown in many ways and particularly by the definition which he offers of the incarnation. 'God's becoming man means that in all Jesus' talk, in his whole proclamation, behaviour and fate, God's word and will have assumed a human form . . . He is in person, is in human form, God's word, will, Son' (DG 685). Such an 'incarnation' of God could be attributed to any prophet, indeed to any religious man. Naturally the pre-existence of Christ (DG 684) and the miraculous birth of Jesus (DG 689) are – incidentally – also denied.

Where the central points of the Christian faith – the Trinity and the mystery of Christ – are uprooted like this, the structure of the building must also collapse. The result is a general falsification of many truths of the Christian faith. Thus there comes a denial of mankind's original condition of supernatural justice, and the rejection of original sin and its transmission. Following current fashion, Küng makes a caricature of the teaching of the Church, when he refers to the true description of the original condition of mankind with phrases like 'golden age', 'mythological fall of man'. Yes, indeed: if someone attacks this caricature, he is merely destroying what is false, and wishes to remedy an evil; but the remedy turns out to be so radical that in the end it destroys the whole vital structure of the truth under discussion. It is true that Küng does not directly contradict the teaching of the Church, for the decisive sentences are kept in question form. Thus, he says of Adam: 'A kind of superman, free from concupiscence, suffering and mortality, endowed with higher knowledge infused by God and with sanctifying grace not only for himself but also for posterity?' (DG 88). Here we have distortions of Church teaching nicely mixed up with correct reports of it. But, nevertheless, the sentence must be judged already wrong, even in this one point alone, where it denies the creation of man in the state of sanctifying grace. This disputing of Church teaching is kept in question form but, even though that is only following Pascal, this makes no actual difference because Küng categorically states 'With regard to the origin and evolution of the world and man, has not science established the very opposite of such a perfect original state?' (DG 88). Here we have also a mistake in method, in that science is set up as the norm for theology and faith. Already at this point it may be remarked that this error about the origin of the world involves consequences for the entire understanding of Christianity in this book: basically Küng does not admit the existence of anything essentially supernatural.

A succinct list of statements in opposition to the teaching of the Church is contained in his criticism of Thomas Aquinas' world picture. He implies (again in question form) that it collapsed as a result of the Copernican revolution, but this 'collapse' affects many truths which are still taught by the Church — 'knowledge of God from the order of creation, . . . the origin and nature of man as consisting in body and soul, original state and original sin, descent of Christ from heaven to earth and to the underworld and his ascension to heaven, grace and seven sacraments . . . end of the world and bodily resurrection from the dead' (DG 36).

Thus a first general survey enables one to recognise that here is a distorted account of the Christian faith. Although in the opinion of theologians, and particularly also in the view of the magisterium, this distortion was already present in *On being a Christian* (and that book was consequently full of errors), something quite new and much more serious has occurred in *Does God exist?* Again and again Küng stresses that his new book should not be separated from the earlier one: 'It is here that the reader will see particularly clearly how little these two books can be separated from each other, how they overlap and are bound to overlap in order to complement and illuminate each other' (DG 566). In view of the premise, confirmed by theologians and by the magisterium of the Church, that *On being a Christian* contains grave errors, these last sentences are an open admission by the author that he has no wish to rectify and correct these errors and that he has on the contrary formally supplemented, broadened and deepened them. The supplementing of an error can only result in a still greater error. In fact in this book there is only a spreading and deepening of his error about the faith.

Am I being over-critical? Let us look at other opinions, including those of Küng's supporters.

The book has in fact had many defenders, even among theologians. D. Emeis called it 'an attempt which deserves great respect' but he extends this praise to the book's central theme, its Christology, warning the reader against taking up a position contrary to Küng's interpretation: 'Anyone who registers doubt . . . ought to read with scrupulous accuracy what the author has to say, for example about Jesus Christ as the "Son of God"'[60] (significantly this reviewer puts the words 'Son of God' in quotation marks, and this can be regarded as an indication that he at any rate is convinced by Küng's 'interpretation-Christ'). He concludes with the usual warning that instead of condemning an opponent one should take seriously his genuineness of purpose. So it is rather a matter of the 'concern' of the other (and who would feel no concern?) and not a question of what is true.

28

H. Verweyen also has a certain sympathy for what is 'not only Küng's longest but also his most valuable book'. Although he goes on to criticise it, his final judgment is one of limited approval: when he says that, in spite of a lack of theological and philosophical accuracy, the book provides a credible answer to modern atheism.[61] All the more positive is the judgment of the media, as when the conclusion is arrived at (a conclusion of significance for the future of the Church) that this book 'will lead to more freedom for young intellectuals'.[62] In general one has the impression that, with the exceptions already mentioned, those who approve of the book find very little to say about its contents. Clearly they are concerned less with what is said in it and more with its effectiveness, its sensational style, form, and journalistic skill. Logically enough: where interest in the truth is low, the attractiveness of the risky and the audacious, and identification with success, have to act as a substitute.

In contrast, the statements by the book's critics are more concerned with what the book actually means, and are the fruit of much toil and thought. That is to be seen in E. von Furstenberg's analysis. He produces evidence that 'in the chaos of Küng's thinking' not only the dogma that God can be known by reason through the revelation of him in nature, but also the Christian concept of God ('No God without the world'), sink in the whirlpool of pantheism.[63] He also uncovers the most deeply concealed fallacy of Küng's whole theory -- the abolition of supernatural reality: 'He dissolves nature into supernature'.[64] K. Krenn identifies a profound lack in the overworked 'fundamental confidence in reality': he finds it unproved, unsupported and aimless. As a result God must be abruptly introduced as a *deus ex machina*. Küng is forced to use God as a stopgap. 'Küng in practice does not go any further than Feuerbach: that is the real, fundamental defect in this book'.[65]

The philosophical weaknesses of Küng's whole approach is also uncovered by M. Baumgartner, althouth he is generous in his recognition of the book as a literary achievement. But 'the train of the philosophical argument in this long book [is] not immediately clear'.[66] In fact there are actually logical gaps at decisive points in its criticism of nihilism.

In one place Küng says that nihilism is self-contradictory; yet he also says that this is not so for the nihilist, since the nihilist holds nihilism to be meaningless and without value. Baumgartner rightly objects that Küng is not distinguishing here between the actual utterance of a statement and its meaning.

Again, the 'fundamental confidence' is claimed by Küng to be superior to the 'fundamental lack of confidence'. Baumgartner asks: 'Is this superiority really due to the fact that the confidence can be carried through logically and consistently? Does not the fundamental lack of confidence also give an access to reality which in its turn can be logically and consistently carried through?' In the process of argument, as Küng develops it, 'the lack of confidence gives just as much access to reality — understood as neutral — only in a different manner'.

But above all Baumgartner criticises the relation of the 'fundamental confidence' to 'confidence in God' — a relation which remains obscure: 'Is the confidence that God exists once more a confidence in the fundamental confidence? Or is it the fundamental confidence itself, only now reflected on itself — or in whatever way one may understand it?'

Finally, Baumgartner asks: 'What argumentative force is there in Küng's reflections, which are intended to show that, if God exists, he is the answer to the fundamental uncertainty of reality? Here lie concealed the decisive systematic difficulties of Küng's line of argument': since the uncertainty of reality is assuredly not removed by belief in God. This is already obvious in the case of the problem of evil in the world. In fact the Christian God is not a kind of totalisator to account for the unintelligible world. In this way he is after all pushed once more into the role of a stopgap.

W. Averbeck analyses the theology of the book.[67] According to him, Küng cannot disentangle himself from the accusation of irrationalism by constantly appealing to the 'fundamental confidence in reality', and must end up in what is called 'fideism'. But even in the all-important Christological problem, Küng is unable to reach the Christ of faith; he reaches only a product of interpretation, a model constructed out of his own intellectual resources. This is a mortally sick theology and the infection, Averbeck says, has already had widespread effects.

From a completely different point of view, H. Albert, who is not a Christian and is a representative of 'critical rationalism', has shown the utterly fatal logical weaknesses in the book. Anyone who praises the book as a great scientific achievement cannot ignore the criticism of this theoretician of science. His is the sharpest and most decisive criticism which has yet been levelled against the book from the standpoint of scientific theory. Albert's objections are important for two reasons: firstly, they show that Küng's proofs that belief in God makes sense fail completely to convince a modern thinker who defends atheism as a possible option for mankind. He sees Küng's concept of God as something constructed from certain a *priori* postulates, used to explain uncertain and meaningless reality.[68] A construction of this kind is wishful thinking, and says nothing about the existence of God. At best it is the achievement of a definition, surely not a very convincing definition; since it is rigged up in such a rhetorical style, that the author himself does not even become aware of its peculiar nature.[69]

Secondly, Albert's analysis of Küng's language is worth noting. He holds that the books *On being a Christian* and *Does God exist?* use a 'copious' and 'vague' vocabulary, that they give 'the impression of a considerable lack of thought'[70] and that the piling up of words conceals rather than solves the problems. Moreover, this rationalistic critic shows a community with Küng in his way of thinking: they have the same views about atrocities in the history of Christianity and about the manifold failures of the Church – a macabre compliment for Küng. In general Albert is sympathetic to Küng's attempt to break out of orthodoxy and counts it to his credit that he has with his concept of God adapted himself to modern views. To be sure, he thinks that the achievements of Küng's thought are weak and that this is merely concealed by an 'enormous vocabulary'. Critical remarks like 'a balancing act in ecclesiastical politics', 'a failure in interpretation', 'a salad of concepts'[71] that is a feature of modern Catholic theology: these remarks are indeed not entirely free from rhetoric, but nevertheless and not without justification, they put Küng's claim to scientific importance in proper perspective. It is difficult also to argue with Albert's assertion that 'the threadbare constructions' are largely directed to readers 'whose intellectual resistance is so weak that he [Küng] can get away with this sort of thing'.[72] Finally, this criticism forces one to think that a theology of this kind compromises the faith rather than helps it. Although Küng presents his book as an exercise in serious theology (and obviously everything which Küng does not accept is not serious), in Albert's view it is unserious and trivial. This opinion is noteworthy, since it shows that the book, in its attempt to attract, does not touch the critical opponent of Christianity, or the atheist (contrary to the optimistic claims which are frequently made). It is obvious that they trust this exaggerated claim to modernity still less, and are even less attracted by it, than by a straightforward theology of a positive faith.

Thus, even a limited selection of views of *Does God exist?* shows that it is rejected by many independent writers. For believing Catholics – occasionally described as 'naive Christians' (DG 637) – the arrogance lies particularly in Küng's constant demand for a change of course, a change which is intended to put the whole life of the Church into reverse gear; it would suppress the 'mistaken decision of the encyclical *Humanae Vitae*' (incidentally Küng naturally does not mention that a growing number even from the medical profession agree with the encyclical) and rejects the magisterium's documents on doctrine concerning the devil and on sexuality, and the prohibition of the ordination of women (DG 117). The whole teaching of the Faith about infallibility (DG 111), God, original sin, the descent and ascension of Christ, the last things: all these must be affected by the new change of course, on account of the modern world picture (DG 115) (which is nowhere properly defined). The 'beatific vision' also (DG 519), the distinction between natural and supernatural (irrelevantly written off as two-storeyed thinking: (DG 518), the so-called 'consolation' of the next life (DG 255), the obligation of absolute norms for inter-personal relations: all this is sacrificed to the change of course. A 'course correction' is also demanded with regard to ideas which the Church never put forward — the 'Credo quia absurdum' (DG 308) or the hostility of the Church to science (Küng would quote Vatican I as an example).

To sum up my own theological judgment with the criticisms which have been made from all these diverse sources: the conclusion is unavoidable that the explanation, elucidation and expansion promised by Küng is entirely consistent with his earlier position. But since that already contains serious errors, the new book has in fact brought about only a widening and deepening of the error. Küng, who was not prepared to correct the mistaken theses of the first book, is only compounding his errors in the second.

3

CRUMBLING FOUNDATIONS

On being a Christian and *Does God exist?* claim to be written on a very high scientific level, and to contain the new theology, which alone is still capable of attracting modern man.

However, a closer examination of these works suggests that this new theology lacks secure foundations, and that in consequence it promotes the growth of many theological diseases which were thought to have been eradicated long ago – even the disease of unrestrained polemic.

In his books Küng often demands tolerance for himself and for other religions (even including the world-outlook of the nihilist and the atheist). But when it comes to his own Chruch, he takes up a position of irreconcilable intolerance. The institutional Church of today and the Church as it is (particularly the Catholic Church) are said in *On being a Christian* (with many ironical and sarcastic remarks) to have no claim to the protection of toleration, since the Church of modern times has compromised the Christian message (Chr 35). Christianity today deserves to be called 'parrot-like Christianity' (Chr 123) on account of its immaturity. In the past, the Church has preached love but sown hatred (Chr 170). In it, dogma, canon law and politics play a more important role than Jesus (Chr 513). It is one of the 'subcultures' and 'organisations living in the past and unaware of the needs of today' (Chr 519).

Theologians not devoted to modernity, as prescribed in these books, are defenders of 'neo-Scholastic Denzinger theology (Chr 33) now abandoned', or are at best 'moderately modern 'theologians' who sometimes seem to be more concerned about formulas and their own petty systems' (Chr 519). Practising Christians, not ready for the change to modernity, are a fear-ridden lot, immature and uncritical in their beliefs (Chr 519). Roman procedures in questions of doctrine are to be considered as 'Inquisition politics' (Chr 687). One is not therefore surprised that Küng concludes that the 'Church is not only far behind the times' (Chr 521) but has also and more importantly 'fallen far short of its own mission' (Chr 521).

Does God exist? also is dominated by one theme which runs right through Küng's work – the failure, extending through all its history, of the

33

Catholic Church and its theology, particularly its failure to recognise and accept the new approaches to the so-called dynamic picture of God, which are contained in the development of philosophy. The author expressly says that he will not write up 'the ecclesiastical *chronique scandaleuse*' (Chr 521). One wonders why a remark of this kind should find place at all in a work about the problem of God. Later it emerges that this remark is meant only as self-protection, to distract attention from the individual items of such a history which are actually contained in the book, only not in historical order. But everything is there which would form part of such a history: Inquisition, burning of heretics (Giordano Bruno), denunciation, erroneous doctrinal decisions, 'narrow-minded, conceited, exclusive particularism' of the Church (DG 594), even a comparison of Catholicism with Communism (DG 325), and above all the unpardonable case of Galileo (DG 9 etc.)! Furthermore, why, in an objective consideration of the problem of God, should personal invective find a place: for instance against the 'court theologians' of the Pope, against Pius XII (DG 117, 519), or against Cardinal Daniélou ('masterly conformist': DG 519)?

In a work written with such personal resentment, in which sarcasm is developed into a regular style, it is not surprising to find that there are serious distortions in even more decisive questions. This is true for the historical question of the relation of faith and science; it is true for the weighty theological problem of the 'two-storeyed doctrine', but particularly for the question of the origin of modern atheism. As regards the first, Küng argues that the breach between reason and faith is due to science (and the wrong attitude of the Church to science); but he misses the mark: the breach had been already prepared by medieval Occamism and was due to philosophical causes. The Galileo case also is to be regarded differently and not as it is depicted in the book with monotonous regularity; at a time when W. Heisenberg has stated, in a wise psychological and historical analysis, 'that in this case each of the two sides could not but think that it was in the right'[73], and when Golo Mann at the international symposium on 'Faith and Science' in Munich (1978)[74] called upon the Church to give up once and for all its Galileo-complex, it just is not good enough to make use of dusty nineteenth century arguments.

If the encyclical *Humanae Vitae* is placed in this list of catastrophes, that is due to an unjustified restriction of the field of vision which pays as little attention to the effect of the encyclical in the Church through the world, as it does to the positive comments which have come from the human sciences.

The most serious mistake is, however, Küng's view that modern atheism derives from the failure of the Church. According to him, the idea 'God over the world' which was put forward in the medieval Church (where was it ever put forward so one-sidedly?) led to deism and to atheism (DG 85, 87, 127). Here the book appropriates, uncritically, Horkheimer's thesis which fits in well with Küng's prejudices. According to Horkheimer, the failure of the Church to put its doctrines into practice made the existence of an infinitely good God impossible to believe (DG 324). Thus, what the humanist Goethe understood to be 'the unique, proper and most profound theme in the history of the world and of mankind', the 'conflict of unfaith with faith', what more recent psychological investigation teaches us to understand as the 'struggle about God'[75] which necessarily accompanies the history of mankind in its damaged state, is here attributed simply to the narrow-mindedness of the Church. But why should anyone become so excited about this, if he regards the Church as a merely human association which assembles around the man Jesus: (cf. Chr 478)?

The question must be asked: Is Küng capable of viewing dispassionately nice distinctions in the context of theological problems; has he the sure hand to direct his thought and its expression? The style of these two books would cause one to wonder. Küng says he wants to introduce a 'radically rational' kind of thinking into theology and into the Church, a thinking and expression which are anything but clear. In fact one can say that in his work lack of clarity and ambiguity are raised to the level of a principle. *On being a Christian* deploys a technique such that each proposition, has with it (either in the context of elsewhere in the book) a counter-proposition with practically the opposite meaning. As a result it is no longer possible to discover exactly what is now the real and final meaning intended by the author.

Here we have that ambiguity in speech and argument which Nietzsche once called 'a blurring of concepts and values and 'fear of every clearcut Yes and No'.[76] This is not the least reason why it is difficult to understand some contemporary theological positions, and these books in particular. For a defender of these books can direct a critic to a counter-quotation for each objection, a quotation which apparently refutes each possible objection. Anyone who objects that in *On being a Christian* the tradition of the Church is misinterpreted or abandoned will be referred to the statement: 'any theologian who neglects this great tradition will pay dearly for it' (Chr 132). If one objects that the substance of the Christian faith is being surrendered in these books, he is told that it is not a clearance sale of Christianity but its reform — as it were, a finer polishing of the 'diamond' (Chr 37). Anyone who voices hesitation and suggests that the doctrine about Christ is being diminished by Küng, will be confronted with a long series of statements to the effect that Jesus is unique, that there is no substitute for him, that no one surpasses him as God's representative — statements which must appear incontestable especially to a layman without training in theology: and in spite of this, the superlatives are neither a summary nor a genuine interpretation of the defined doctrine of the Church, which is that Christ is truly God and truly man in one (divine) person.

To illustrate this sort of thing, let me use Küng's account of the resurrection of Jesus as an example. He wishes to point out with particular emphasis that the resurrection not only shows the importance of the cross (R. Bultmann) and the continuation of the 'cause' of Jesus (W. Marxsen) but also that 'it was certainly (for faith) a real event' (Chr 351). 'The fact that God intervenes at the point where everything is at an end from the human point of view, this – despite the [complete] maintenance of natural laws – is the true miracle of the resurrection: the miracle of the beginning of a new life out of death' (Chr 350). But on account of the parenthesis 'despite the maintenance of the laws of nature', this resurrection is in no way the resurrection of the body taught by the Church. Consequently, Küng also writes off (against all the rules of historical method) the empty grave, as a legendary elaboration of the message of the resurrection which had preceded it (Chr 364).

But 'despite the [complete] maintenance of the laws of nature' the appearances of the risen Jesus to the disciples, which Küng holds to in words, are wrapped in an impenetrable dusk. For this reason he also speaks only of 'accounts of appearances' (Chr 351) and 'statements about appearances' (Chr 364) and for these as well the demand holds, that nothing unusual can have happened in human space and time.

This technique is further developed in *Does God exist?*, probably in order to state the orthodox doctrine about the question of the existence of God with a torrent of words, but in reality to hide it from the unsuspecting reader with this very torrent.

So, for example, when he says of the nihilist that he sees everywhere 'instability, fragility, transitoriness, fleetingness, emptiness, ineffectiveness, discordance, in the last resort uselessness, pointlessness, worthlessness – in a word – nothingness' (DG 419), this is an indiscriminate collection of characteristics that are on different levels and have no intrinsic connection with one another: for the instability, weakness and transitoriness of the world are characteristics which no one can miss, which everyone must recognise and which have nothing to do with any kind of nihilism; whereas the assertion of the absolute worthlessness of the world could certainly be described as nihilistic, if it were really so asserted. But Küng is unable to demonstrate this: his thinking deals with clear alternatives, and in his black and white picture, he takes no account of the possible gradations between the two extremes.

When therefore he describes the statement 'all that is could also not be'

(DG 419) as nihilistic, one must object that this is only the fundamental principle of the limitation and contingency of all finite being, a principle which belongs to the metaphysics which he scorns. Moreover, the many compound words which he forms for the definition of the new conception of God could only impress the sort of reader who from the start renounces all effort to think, and is ready to allow himself to be carried away by waves of rhetoric.

Similarly, there is mention of an unitary understanding of reality within which alone the concept of God is to be accommodated. The author therefore attributes 'secularity' and 'historicity' to God without saying what is the proper meaning of these ideas, which are used to-day in a great many meanings. They can be understood as descriptions of God's activity towards the world, an activity which Christianity with its belief in creation has never denied, and which cannot be claimed as an achievement of modern times. But it is then said of the 'secularity' and 'historicity' of God that both these characteristics are to be understood analogically only, that is, are to be taken as like and unlike the truth (DG 184, 186).

But analogy implies difference of two realities in question, as well as their similarity. So, by speaking of 'analogy' Küng (having previously arged for a unitary understanding of reality – which only a positivist could hold) contradicts himself. This shows that he cannot explain for himself or to his readers the meaning of his ideas. Certainly he does not know how, and does not intend, to give a clear meaning to his statements since they would be in fact to a great extent meaningless. Actually in decisive contexts one finds constantly in Küng whole series of meaningless assertions which were never seriously discussed in theological thought, assertions of this kind: 'God is not an extramundane being, beyond the stars, in a metaphysical heaven. . . . God is not . . . a constitutionally reigning monarch' (DG 185). Such remarks are obviously written for completely uninformed readers.

The treatment of God's 'personality' is one example of the word-play Küng indulges in. Without saying what 'being a person' means, and what more profound meaning is to be inferred in the use of the concept when applied to the trinitarian God, Küng begins with a statement which no one denies: 'God is not a person as man is a person' (DG 632). Then (instead of speaking about analogy) he calls the word 'person' a code word for the fact that 'God is more than person'. But 'God is also not less than a person'. So finally, he is 'neither personal nor nonpersonal, since he is both at once.' Here the illogicality comes to light; for when two characteristics are excluded they cannot again be produced as available at the same time. In the conclusion, however, the assertion is supplemented by the remark that since God is both personal and impersonal, he 'is therefore transpersonal'. Thus the two concepts are first rejected as descriptions of God; then they are both claimed for God, under the label 'trans-personal', which means transcendentally personal: no explanation is given of what this means.

A critic has rightly asked: 'After what the author says here, one could have no hesitation in supposing that what is being discussed here is no longer an idea but only a word to which he cannot give any intelligible meaning. If then this is so, one may ask what view is to be taken of his . . . assertions about the problem of God: Is it not partly a matter not of assertions, but of meaningless statements?'[77] It is not easy to answer this critic.

The lack of clarity in these books appears not only in the outward form of statements and formulations, which catch the untrained reader off guard; it lies deeper in the theological basis of this theologising. Therefore right from the start one can assume that an author who keeps up a continual criticism of the Church and its mission will hardly be able to acknowledge this Church as the immediate norm of faith: as a result, a fundamental principle of theology is lost, and this must have particularly negative effects on one's attitude to Holy Scripture and to its interpretation.

Thus *On being a Christian* starts with the claim that its earth-shaking assertions about Jesus, and about being a Christian, are founded on strict exegetical science, and on the historical-critical method. It criticises those Christians today who 'with astonishing naiveté' . . . 'also know already who and what this Jesus Christ is' (Chr 124) – as if there were no liturgy, no living preaching of the Church and no tradition, which tell the person who is willing to believe, who Christ was, and who he is today and forever (cf. Hebr 13:8). One might simply remark: if after the appearance of Jesus Christ and after almost two thousand years' history of the efficacy of his person and his work, Christendom does not yet know 'who or what this Christ is', then it cannot be helped at this late stage, even by a new attempt at clarification made by an allegedly modern scientific theology which has not fully thought out the problems arising from the historical-critical method.

Küng certainly does claim to be giving this valid, and in his opinion finally valid, explanation. This explanation is to be taken from the actual public history of Jesus of Nazareth as it is written down in the Gospels: for 'with the historical-critical method in this comprehensive sense, theology is provided with an instrument enabling the question about the true, real, historical Christ to be asked in a way that was simply not possible in former centuries' (Chr 156). In fact he also says, in passing, that the Gospels are not simple historical reports and are not biographies of Jesus, but testimonies of believers about Jesus, which in turn are intended to promote faith in him. But what these testimonies then properly produce, and what the author wishes to achieve by means of them, is the purely human history 'of the living Jesus of Nazareth, his words, deeds and sufferings' (Chr 160). He does in fact mention that the Jesus of history should not be separated from the Christ of faith, but he does not keep to this principle. That means that in fact in the book the contribution of faith to the history of Jesus is stripped away and then Jesus is brought forward as a figure of purely human history. The author follows (without formal acknowledgment) the principle laid down by the liberal theologian W. Herrmann (+ 1922) who once avowed: 'We who are seeking redemption through Jesus ought not dare to believe the same lofty things about Jesus as they [the disciples] . . . have believed about him'.[78] It is not only that the Christ defined in the faith of the Church, in the councils and in the piety of the faithful, is rejected. Much more: the Christ believed in by the evangelists is rejected and is replaced by a Jesus of Nazareth who was a mere man, but who is admittedly said to have had (and this alone is conceded) some kind of closer connection with God, the Father. But all these are, however, details and features of a merely human life, and have not the significance taught by supernatural faith. One need not, and indeed cannot, have *faith* in perfectly clear historical facts and persons.

Küng's passing over all the statements and testimonies about Christ which express any higher claim of Jesus Christ to anything 'super-human' or 'divine' shows how fundamentally the faith of the Apostles and of the authors of the New Testament writings is disregarded. The statements about Christ in the Epistle to the Hebrews, about the 'eternal priesthood of Christ' are considered to be of no significance; similarly the statement in St Matthew's Gospel (Mt 11:27) of his union with the Father in knowledge of each other, and their consequent consubstantiality. The book explains this expression of a consciousness on Jesus' part that he is super-human, by saying that this is an enigmatic statement from which one may not conclude to the occurrence of an unique revelation. It is indeed conceded that the early Christian community applied a series of sublime titles to the man Jesus ('the Christ', 'the Messiah', 'the son of David', 'the Son of God'), but at the same time they held firmly that 'Jesus was entirely man' (Chr 286ff).

Their sole object was to underline in this way the importance and value of Jesus and his cause, and to ensure that he continued to be seen as the one who set the standard (Chr 384). But here also one asks: What was the basis of this standard, if Jesus were after all only a man? In this context Küng can only mean that, for this Christian community as well, Jesus was no more than a mere man. (Again the question arises: Can one, may one, have *faith* in a mere man?) Küng, in what he claims to be a procedure of scientific exegetics, passes over not merely the highly theological assertions of Paul and John about the person of Jesus and his divinity, but also pays no attention to the investigations of serious modern exegesis. This exegesis is able to show with good reason that the title 'Son of God' in the New Testament (and this is already true for Mark and the Synoptics: cf. for example Mk 1:11; 9:7; 12:6; Mt 16:17) unites 'the person Jesus with God' and that this apparently dogmatic information can be proved 'with good historical reasons'.[79] These and other descriptions are not inventions of hellenism and 'not mythical symbols' (as asserted in Chr 388) but they are 'logically developed rather than mythological' and are the result of 'Christological thinking brought to a final logical conclusion'. Anyone who takes refuge in myth at this point must listen to the Evangelical exegete M. Hengel: 'The apparently scientific, but often really merely superficial, dismissal of such statements as mythological could at times be also an indication of intellectual simplicity and indolence'.[80]

The final question to be asked about an exegesis of this kind is how a theologian who does not acknowledge the inspiration of Holy Scripture and does not share the belief of the Church of today about these texts can reach their truth and find their real meaning. One must certainly also take into consideration that the author is not aware of the indissoluble unity of Scripture, tradition and the Church, which is an essential point in Catholic theology. Who then provides the necessary religious understanding of these texts, texts which must in fact present a particular history not confined solely to this world? The book does not clarify this essential question of procedure and method, a question which is vital when one is dealing scientifically with Holy Scripture (a title which he feels to be inappropriate: Küng claims that he is pursuing 'serious biblical criticism': Chr 465f). Küng wishes to raise 'a methodical counterquestion from the testimonies of faith [contained in Scripture] to the historical Jesus' (Chr 159). The result should be, he says, the discovery of an authentic portrait of the historical Jesus, which should not however resemble the nineteenth century liberal portrayals of Jesus (Chr 158). Neither should one begin with a particular modern portrayal of Jesus. Fundamentally, historical science should determine the exegesis. Yet he concedes that this science can bring to light only probabilities when dealing with the Bible (Chr 158).

Distrust of the possibility of a historical reconstruction of the historical Jesus appears quite clearly in Küng's statement that a 'saying put into Jesus' mouth by the evangelist – and therefore "unauthentic" – can just as authentically reproduce the authentic Jesus as a saying which he himself really uttered – and therefore "authentic"'(Chr 159) since it is a question of the so-called 'open total picture'. But how can such an 'open total picture' be surely obtained, if the details are already unattainable? In this regard Küng is in fact clearly not really serious about the historical-critical method. Finally, he admits that Christianity is not merely concerned with Jesus 'as he really was' (Chr 160), that is with the historical Jesus. Yet he had expressly stated that this was the objective of exegesis. It is a matter, then, of Jesus 'as he confronts us here and now' (Chr 160). One must put the further question: From where does one get the norm which shows that the 'Jesus who meets us here and now' is the true Jesus? This norm cannot be derived from the Church, interpreting Holy Scripture and teaching the truth about Jesus, since the Church has been written off as an official interpreter of Scripture. Neither can it come from the faith of the original community and of the biblical writers, since they have overpainted the picture of Jesus with their mythical conceptions. Thus we must conclude that neither historical science, nor the faith of the original community, nor the teaching of the Church can provide the norm for the correct understanding of the real Jesus. How then does the book justify its claim to come in contact with the historical Jesus? Dare one simply say: not at all!

Küng's apparent attempt at a proof points in fact in the direction of a merely subjective account of Jesus which depends on current fashions. For the subjectivist attitude can be cited his statement: 'He [the author, and the reader of the Bible] allows himself to be inspired by the Spirit of this Scripture' (Chr 467), that is, he interprets it through his own experience and on his own authority. But since a man who proceeds with such complete subjectivism can hardly expect to find a hearing among his contemporaries, the 'present state of man and society' must be brought in for good measure (Chr 160). This means nothing less than that his picture of Jesus is constructed to fit in with the interests and feelings of the contemporary society. This demonstrates the inadequacy of Küng's method and the weakness of his subjective exegesis, and of his whole theological work. One can rather come to the conclusion (and the continuance in *On being a Christian* of what is here begun makes it a certainty) that from this 'Jesus of modern society' no values are to be learned which modern society does not already recognise, such as human solidarity, freedom from pressure to consumption, quality of life etc. The picture of Jesus is already established even before a single line is drawn, and at the end no social value is learned which had not been known already.

According to the author this subjective treatment of Holy Scripture is the result of a strict adherence to the historical-critical method and biblical exegesis: in fact, he has reproached his critics for not having 'proper appreciation of an exegesis which is based on logical historical criticism.'[81]

In the later book also (*Does God exist?*) he includes, among the individual elements of the radical change of course, a demand that the historical-critical method should have absolute validity for the interpretation of Holy Scripture. One of the first signs of the 'transition to maturity' in theology is the 'adoption of the modern world picture and development of the historical-critical method' (DG 111). Thus, after an explanation of the Trinity which he has derived entirely from his own individual presuppositions, he criticises (in question form) the later councils of the Church: 'Is it not more understandable, more illuminating, than the many speculations of later times – often very remote from the New Testament and little more than pure philosophizing – on the one divine nature . . . in the three Persons. . . ?' (DG 701).

In this not only is the Church denied the right to give an authentic interpretation of Holy Scripture, and its doctrinal definitions pushed into the category of mere speculation, but these words also show a complete misunderstanding of the relevance of the historical-critical method for theology, and for exegesis in particular, insofar as it lays claim to being a scientific account of the faith. Küng here takes no account of the limitations of this method set by modern exegesis itself, which is always self-critical. He adheres instead to an entirely naïve use of this method.

In fact, a critical use of it must pay practical attention to the fact that no supernatural truth and no fact concerning salvation can be grasped by using the historical-critical method which is essentially based on the principle that all historical developments come about from natural causes, on their context inside the world, and on the possibility of proving them logically. This is not to deny the importance of this method in the interpretation of the Bible, considered as a book composed by men: but because of its rational and technical nature, it cannot take in and transmit any belief in a supernatural mystery. For this reason, exegesis through historical criticism has a very significant function, in that it can explain the natural and historical causes of Scripture, and the presuppositions for the understanding of its content by faith. But it cannot of itself make any binding declarations about the faith. As a science, it must of course also recognise that its judgments are, in principle, no more than assertions of probability and, in principle, subject to revision, while faith always produces knowledge which gives certainty, and cannot prove fallacious.

For this reason exegesis is not a norm or rule of faith. Without any diminishing of its value as a science, it must relinquish this authority to the Church, which has been endowed with the teaching authority of Christ. Since, however, *On being a Christian* and *Does God exist?* quite overtly aim at being a sort of counter-tribunal to the authority of the Church, they fail to recognise essential findings of Catholic doctrinal principles in the interpretation of Scripture as well. One can quite justly say that the theology they propose rests on entirely false presuppositions – at least to the extent that the author wishes to feel himself associated with the Catholic principle of faith.

This applies also to Küng's appeal to the modern world picture which is still determined by the intellectual outlook of the nineteenth century, quite in the sense of Rudolf Bultmann. With regard to Küng's somewhat casual remarks about the new world picture which faith must use, one could bring in the authority — not lightly to be dismissed — of Karl Jaspers. Jaspers once rightly declared that the modern view was exactly characterised by the fact that it has to renounce the possibility of an unitary world picture. Only 'a pseudo-science, which is on the contrary the average enlightenment of all ages'[82], makes such a claim. One can however go further and point to the statements of natural science, such as what P. Jordan says: The thesis that 'for scientific thought the world and its history are a closed system' is 'quite simply false'.[83] This modern physicist, who is expert particularly in problems on the boundaries of science, adds the still more important statement: it is possible that 'the sphere of religious thought can be reconciled with the natural sciences of today without any logical contradiction'.[84] For this reason the surrender, demanded in *Does God exist?*, of decisive doctrines of the Catholic faith for the sake of the new world picture, is quite unjustified. It could already have been rejected on the grounds that these truths — the Trinity, the divinity of Christ, the virgin birth, the resurrection — were denied even in the world of antiquity, and that the true faith had been exposed to contradiction then just as it is now. It is thus possible that the faith be accepted or rejected in one and the same world picture. In that fact there already is an indication that the faith is not dependent on the current world picture, since a world picture is only an approximately successful piecing together of all the scientific data which lie on the horizontal level of experience, while faith opens to mankind a new vertical dimension which rises above every world picture. This dimension can, on the one hand, be open to objection in every world picture, but on the other hand it can also be held to be completely without contradiction, once it is properly explained.

In saying this, one grants, of course, something which Küng does not allow to a theological system which holds fast to the faith of the Church: that the faith makes use of elements for its expression which are conditioned by the world, and uses formulations which must be remodelled in a new historical situation. This constitutes the task of interpretation of the old formulations of the faith, a task widely taken in hand by modern hermeneutics. But one cannot simply say of these old formulations that they are no longer intelligible: in that case one would obviously not have been able to 'interpret' and 'translate' them.

Küng's interest — stressed again and again — lies in this task of 'interpretation' and 'translation'. For this reason he says repeatedly: 'Now we must interpret'.[85] 'For me belief in the incarnation is a matter of interpretation'.[86] But in doing this he fails to notice that he takes no serious account of the fact that we are not asked to believe interpretations (above all, those of any individual theologian or group of theologians); faith, on the contrary, is directed to the content and meaning of its authentic declarations as proposed to the faithful by the Church (cf. DS 3020). This meaning must therefore be accurately reproduced by every interpretation. This is not only a requirement of Church teaching; it is also demanded by modern hermeneutics, which obviously strives to ensure that the original meaning be expressed undiminished, and as far as possible in a better way. H. G. Gadamer has therefore demanded that the explanation or interpretation of an original work must adhere to the following principle: 'Explanation does not wish to replace the work which is explained. It does not, for example, wish to attract attention to itself through the poetical force of its own expression. It has a fundamentally accidental character'[87], that is, it wishes to serve the original with complete loyalty, and enable it to have undiminished effect in the new situation. A correct explanation must therefore be always able to demonstrate that the new interpretation reproduces the original without falsification, that it has therefore been 'correctly' made. In the case of Küng one has the contrary impression – that every interpretation is already valid simply because it has been made at all. It is like when no distinction is made any more between a correct copy and a distortion. Küng makes no allowance for the possible occurrence of distortion.

You can test this with a simple example of the doctrine about Christ, and ask if the formula 'Christ is God and man in one divine Person' has the same meaning as the interpretation 'Christ is God's attorney for men'. Every intelligent man will understand that this is a plain misinterpretation.

Since Küng assumes without question the true agreement of his interpretation with the 'original', his hermeneutic procedure must be regarded as insufficient and inadmissible. In fact here is no exact and disciplined interpreting: without it being tested, he claims his interpretation is truth, and forces it upon the inexperienced reader. Similarly, subjective impressions and loose paraphrases are produced as originals. Even in this essential matter of the faithful translation of the title-deeds of Christianity the foundations of his method are seen to be crumbling.

4

A NEW WAY TO GOD
OR A THEOLOGICAL
CUL-DE-SAC?

The principal concern of *Does God exist?* is to bring about a correction of course in the whole approach to the question of God; in particular it aims at getting rid of the 'antiquated image of God' (DG 182), 'the naïve anthropomorphic understanding of God' (DG 184), so as to attain 'a modern, secular understanding of God' (DG 185) which can attract the nihilist and the atheist. Looked at from this point of view one can understand its dedication 'ad maiorem Dei gloriam' and the creed-like ending: 'In you, Lord, I have hoped, I shall never be put to shame' (DG 702). Given such a confession of faith, whose personal sincerity is not to be doubted, the question arises: Should we not let Küng be?; should we not be quite happy with a testimony of this kind?

A negative answer can come only from one who is convinced that there is a specifically Christian and Catholic faith in God, which is not reached by every confession of faith. Catholic faith cannot be a private individual faith; it is legitimate, only if it is a faith shared with the community of faith which is the Church. It is precisely when a belief in God is proposed as being new and revolutionary, that it needs to be tested before the forum of the thinking faith of the Church.

This is all the more true because Küng claims his new conception of God has been arrived at in a new way, and established by a new method. Questions regarding method (or way: method is 'the way of investigating') certainly belong in a special manner to theology. In the matter of the 'way to God' or of the 'knowledge of God' the Church has actually bound itself by solemn definitions (in Vatican I). This was obviously done in the knowledge that this question was important for the true faith; for, in fact, the way one enters on the subject determines the goal arrived at – true or erroneous faith in God.

The determination of this new way to the knowledge of God is essentially the chief concern of *Does God exist?*; it is all about the 'way of critical rationality', in particular the way 'of radical rationality'. Nevertheless this way must not, Küng says, end in rationalism. Neither should it coincide with

45

the teaching of the Church about the natural knowledge of God derived from created things with the help of the light of natural reason (cf. Vatican I: DS 3004).

This matter was already touched on in *On being a Christian*. Küng there wishes to proceed very critically, and begins with Kant's objections to the proofs of God's existence. (In the course of this, he incorrectly connects 'practical reason', which in Kant means the 'purely moral will', with human activity, and thus completely fails to recognise that 'practical reason' is also autonomous human reason and implies a genuine knowledge.) He wishes 'to place (every man) before a rationally responsible decision (in favour of the reality of God': Chr 69). But in plain contradiction to this he says, some pages later, that it is not possible either to refute atheism or give a rational proof of belief in God (Chr 74). For this reason, the ultimate justification of belief in God is 'a confidence grounded on reality itself' (Chr 74). Appropriately, he adds that 'atheism and belief in God are ventures (and) . . . risks' (Chr 74). This means that the author is not exactly facing men with 'a decision which can be rationally responsible', but with a call to a 'fundamental trust', 'a basic confidence' in reality, a confidence which naturally the non-Christian can also have; he obstructs the approach of reason towards faith (since no one makes a demand for a formal proof). What then can he mean when he says, yet again, that he is engaged in 'critical examination' of belief in God? A theologian who regards belief as just as unprovable as unbelief reduces the decision about faith to a game of chance with two completely equal possibilities. There is this difference, but it is not essential in the argument, that in this lottery there are only two tickets. Because the justification of belief is reduced to a subjective primary confidence, Küng takes away the ground from under scientific theology: for no science can be built on a belief that is no more than a 'venture' and a 'risk'.

In saying this Küng draws down on himself unanimous criticism from modern philosophers of science: they reproach modern theology precisely for its 'tendency to immunise' itself against the demands for a reasoned guidance towards belief. Anyone who is not able to give any reasonable criteria for the so-called 'primary confidence' and then assures us that while the person is producing this confidence he immediately grasps its justification, breaks off all discussion about the reasonable presuppositions of belief, and is furthermore unable to distinguish this 'primary confidence' from self-deception.

The incoherence of this attempt to develop a new doctrine about the knowledge of God becomes particularly clear in two passages. It comes first in the debate with atheism. Since in fact reality seems to the atheist to be extremely doubtful, and since it appears to have no primary basis or primal purpose, it gives him an occasion for denying God's existence: 'atheism cannot be eliminated rationally' (Chr 73). But later Küng says that atheism is not able 'to suggest any condition for the possibility of uncertain reality' (Chr 75) and therefore it lacks a radical rationality (Chr 75) and fundamentally surrenders to an 'irrational trust in human reason' (Chr 75). But if, in any debate, one has shown one's opponent that he cannot justify his intellectual position, that in fact he is proceeding irrationally, this means that he has been shown to have serious inconsistencies in his reasoning, and in this sense his position has been refuted.

Küng's interpretation of reality is also inconsistent. At one point he says reality is totally doubtful and unfounded: but at another it is said to provide in itself an 'ultimate foundation, support and meaning' (Chr 74f). Is reality really split in two like this, split into the meaningless and the significant? If it really were so divided, how could one say to the atheist that he is acting irrationally, when he refuses to trust this reality; and how could one summon the believer to a trust in reality, if it is hopelessly divided in this way, and since, in this very trust, he would have to say 'yes' also to the divided reality?

But at this point in the argument, the higher rationality of the fundamental trust in reality and as well of the acceptance of God is supposed to have been demonstrated. This is done by the simple assertion that 'ultimate reality, in a variety of ways, challenges me to accept it' (Chr 76), and that this acceptance is altogether 'the right thing' do to, 'in fact the most sensible thing of all' (Chr 77), since it is only in this way that the inexplicable world is explained and its uncertainty resolved. Here Küng certainly forgets to say that the atheist also can offer such an explanation (as for example Engels, by referring to the eternal circulation of matter) and that any thinker in this situation would be obliged to investigate this solution with his powers of reason. It must have been possible to distinguish clearly the concept of 'the most reasonable of all reasons' from the less perfect, and to demonstrate that the higher reason is superior to the lower. But that would go in the direction of a proof of God's existence based on reason, a thing which modern thought allegedly does not contemplate.

For this reason Küng leaves aside the 'most reasonable reason of all' and puts the emphasis on an act of decision and confidence, an act which has no 'extrinsic rationality' but only a so-called 'intrinsic rationality' proper to itself (Chr 77), which establishes its own certainty in its actual accomplishments and therefore experimentally. But since this confidence must not be preceded by reason, the venture involved in this trust or belief (since belief in God is here broadly equated with 'basic confidence') is in the end not accounted for; since only a spiritual being can give such an account, and then only by the application of reason.

Probably suspecting the inconsistency and incoherence of this way towards the acceptance of God, Küng, in *Does God exist?*, tackles the problem once more, in greater breadth and detail. But you cannot correct an error merely by extending it. Certainly, for the Catholic theologian, it is significant and obvious that, in the question of the natural knowledge of God, Küng decidedly departs from the teaching of the Vatican I (a teaching repeated by Vatican II).[88] The binding declaration of the Council, which Küng himself also cites, is as follows: 'Whoever says that the one true God, our Creator and Lord, cannot be surely known by the natural light of human reason, is to be shunned' (DS 3026). Küng inadmissibly translates 'anathema sit' as 'let him condemned', which runs contrary to the normal forms of expression of a council, since the Church never pronounces a final sentence of damnation against anyone. At first this judgment is only described as a 'harsh theological proposition' (DG 510). But in what follows rhetorical questions are used to cast doubt on its validity: 'an ingenious solution to the problem of reason and faith?' (as if councils ever sought to give patent solutions); 'Is it a bad or a fair compromise?' (DG 513). In his answer he does not say it is a 'bad compromise', yet speaks of 'a superficial juxtaposition of reason and faith' (DG 513f). He goes on to report fully 'the theologically most important attack on the definition of Vatican I' (DG 514), made by the Protestant theologian Karl Barth. He calls Barth's rejection of the Council 'marvellously consistent' (DG 517). As well, although he does not fully support this statement and its opposition to 'natural theology' (surely not least because the whole tendency of his book is in the direction of a purely natural theology), he nevertheless joins in criticism of Vatican I and its 'two-level reality' (DG 522), as if nature and grace must be thought of as forming a two-storeyed building. His fundamental denial of the difference between nature and grace, and between the two differing orders of knowledge, which appears here, leads finally to his abandonment of Vatican I, expressed in the proposition: 'the right way would lie ... between Karl Barth and Vatican I' (DG 536).

But now the circular thinking begins again; not starting with reason, he tries to establish that 'fundamental trust in reality' can be a substitute for the allegedly rationalistic knowledge of God taught by the Church, and that it can produce a 'radical rationality' (DG 572) and a radical reasonableness.

If one expects at this decisive point to learn something about the character, kind and nature of this fundamental trust, a trust not derived from reason and still described as being 'rational' (but again not 'rationalistic'), a trust demanding a decision of the will (which yet must not be 'irrational'), a trust which contains, once it is achieved, all the ambiguity, uncertainty and insecurity of reality (so that eventually faith and disbelief always exist side by side), one does not escape from the logical dilemma.

To try to do justice to Küng, one can clear away, from the basic structure of this new way to God, the masses of words piled needlessly one on another, and express it as follows: the approach to God must start from the present reality, since, because a distinction between the natural and the supernatural is denied, there can be only one reality. This reality is, however, very profoundly uncertain, 'suspended between being and not being, evolving without aim' (DG 566). But 'if God exists' this groundless and empty reality receives a 'primal meaning, primal value' (DG 567). Yet there also proceeds from this reality (which has been described as so disunited) a strong impulse to trust. As far as atheism is concerned 'it cannot prevail against such confidence imposed on us in the light of reality itself' (DG 569). Reality is therefore simultaneously doubtful and trustworthy, but its trustworthiness obviously exercises a more powerful force. Nevertheless, men do not follow this more powerful attraction through seeing that it is reasonable; no: they must willingly decide in favour of it, antecedently to all perception of its reasonableness. But how can such a decision or a confidence of this kind be defended, if reason is not already part of the whole process?

Obviously Küng cannot deny the influence of reason on the occurrence of such a decision of the will, leading to confidence – for he constantly says that this decision is confirmed, whereas the opposite decision he declares to be groundless. But the discovery of a reason, or the procedure for getting this confirmation, is still a process of intellectual perception, involving the use of reason. If, then, the influence of reason is to be excluded from the process of confirmation, then Küng is not justified in speaking of 'well-founded fundamental confidence', nor in attributing to the atheist an 'unfounded confidence' in reality. If reason does not play a part, confidence in reality cannot be described as well-founded. All he is left with is an unfounded irrational confidence.

His further development of this idea shows that this interpretation is correct. His objective is to assert that the reasonableness of this confidence appears first while it is actually being achieved. 'If I dare to apply myself and give myself up to (reality), then I know not indeed before, nor yet only afterward, but by the very act of doing this, that I am doing the right thing and even what is absolutely the most reasonable thing. For what cannot be proved in advance, I experience in the accomplishment, in the very act of acknowledging what I perceive' (DG 573).

Philosophical critics of this approach, itself described as philosophic, have rightly seen essential inconsistencies in it. They have pointed out that in any case the beginning of this way to God is quite arbitrary, since man has already set out on his journey when he first perceives that 'the haze is clearing',[89] whereas the key question is: Can man justify rationally the first step on the journey? If this step is made without justification and irrationally, everything that follows later is equally to be labelled irrational.

The appeal to experience (which comes next in Küng's presentation) is particularly questionable, since he elsewhere explains that God is not an object of 'immediate experience' (DG 575). But still here he is said to be experienced! Küng's answer amounts to this: man actually experiences the primal support and the primal meaning! But this means that he still doesn't answer the question about possible delusion; he simply repeats his questionable thesis, and at the same time asserts that men become conscious at this point of the 'radical rationality' of their trust in God (DG 572). Philosophers have justly pointed out that the 'logical justification of the basic confidence is simply missing'[90] and that this 'philosophical section of the book is disappointing.'[91] The basis of the confidence is the confidence itself, that is: it is a baseless confidence.

This central thesis of the book is refuted also by M. Baumgartner. It practically amounts, he says, to an assertion that basic confidence is preferable to basic lack of confidence, because it can be carried through theoretically and practically. But we can quite properly ask: 'Does basic lack of confidence not also give access to reality, an access which can for its part be consistently and logically carried through?'[92] The assertion that reality remains a closed book to the basic lack of confidence (or, to put it concretely, to a person who does not take the first step towards the 'Yes') can only be made when one regards reality right from the beginning as endowed with meaning (and can support this view), that is, when one attributes meaning to reality before taking the first step towards the experience of confidence. But this can happen only with the help of reason.

So, no matter where this chain of thought is taken up, it nowhere shows genuine continuity or coherence. Consequently, a representative of critical rationalism says that Küng's way of proving God's existence 'is like a patchwork quilt, displaying all colours', and 'that even in the framework of his own presuppositions – within his intellectual horizon – his line of argument fails to hold'.[93] As a result H. Albert speaks of an 'underhand way to God'.

Measured by the standard of the teaching of the faith (Vatican I), such a way of producing faith (which moreover does not distinguish between natural and supernatural knowledge of God) cannot be regarded as justified by reason. The Church emphasises the possibility of a reasoned approach to a natural knowledge of God, precisely on the ground of human responsibility (DS 3004): but Küng sacrifices this in favour of a choice by the will, a choice said to be guaranteed by a postulated experience of its evidence. Furthermore, this attempt cannot escape the suspicion of 'irrationalism' and of a 'fideism' which eliminates reason; nor can it find any support in Holy Scripture (Rom 1:18-20: DG 524ff).

Thus one must also say that Küng's approach does not take account of the declarations of the faith. When, for example, Vatican II says that 'God, who has created and preserves all things through the Word, gives man a continual testimony of himself in created realities'[94], it is speaking not of the intellect taken in isolation, but of the spiritual nature of the whole man, who as a spiritual being is open for the testimony of God and can assure himself of this openness by a process of thought. Seen in this light the proofs of God's existence (when one distinguishes their traditional form from the meaning they contain) acquire lasting importance: through a process of thought they render visible, in this finite world, absolute Truth and Goodness. Genuine philosophic thinking can, even today, hold what these proofs contain of eternal philosophy, yet Küng seems to dismiss them.[95]

It is possible to show more precisely that the way begun by Küng not only is tangled and confused but also does not lead to a God of faith and revelation. This is apparent when he tries to bring together the basic confidence and God himself. In *On being a Christian* he once says casually that 'this trusting commitment to an ultimate basis, support and meaning of reality is itself rightly designated in general usage, as "belief" in God ("faith in God," "trust in God")'∷ Chr 74. He says in fact that 'basic trust and belief in God' ("trust in God") have [only] an analogous structure' (Chr 78). But he does not succeed in tracing an essential difference between the two, between faith and trust. This is also easy to understand, since he does not recognise the reality of the supernatural.

Consequently it has been rightly asked how this confidence that reality in general makes sense, a confidence which is also possible (though without reason) for the atheist, is related to confidence about God's existence, that is, to a proper belief in God, a belief in the absolute meaning of reality. Is confidence that God exists once again a confidence in the basic confidence? or is it the basic confidence itself, only reflected in itself? In fact the two are not to be distinguished: since 'affirmation of God implies an ultimately justified fundamental confidence' (DG 572). 'If someone affirms God, he knows why he can trust reality'(DG 572); but apart from the fact that he cannot 'know' this, since he has established or postulated it by a decision of the will, it also becomes clear from the statement that what is here in question is a God who is identical with the ultimate basis of reality. At any rate it is not the God of supernatural Christian belief in revelation.

It is therefore not surprising that at the end of this road which finishes in a cul-de-sac we find, not the supernatural God of the trinitarian mystery, but a philosophical concept of a God partly identical with the world. Already in his statements in *On being a Christian* about the relationship of Jesus with God, it is striking how critically Küng regards the 'concept of Father' in reference to God. The assertion that Jesus made no real change in the belief in God found in the Old Testament, and that 'certainly the originality of Jesus . . . should not be exaggerated' (Chr 299) comes as no surprise. In harmony with this is his unconcealed sympathy for the rigid unitarianism of Islam with its emphasis on 'the one God and his legate' (Chr 113). But a monotheism of Hegel's type (modern thought apparently does not go back further than Hegel: Chr 448) can naturally not be conceived in the sense of the faith of the Church. This is the impression given by formulations found already in *On being a Christian*: 'Man is in God and God is in man'. As a result the 'history of man is taken up in the history of God' (Chr 377). The usual Hegelianism which shows through here comes out even more clearly in *Does God exist?*

That book shows at first a strong tendency to approve of the monotheism frequently found in the history of religions and which is described as being also an essential characteristic of biblical faith in God. But after this not only is the concept of person a victim of criticism (DG 631) but the living God of Pascal ('God of Abraham, Isaac and Jacob') is also described as an 'antiquated image of God' (DG 182). The new picture of God is now presented, more clearly than in *On being a Christian*, as a Hegelian variation of the God who is dependent on history, who comes to himself in history. 'A correlation must be asserted between God and man' (DG 183). This correlation, however, should not involve any equalisation or identification: 'There must be no equation of God and man. Even though God and man are not to be separated from each other, neither are they to be identified' (DG 183). But this non-identification cannot correct and remove the error involved in proposing the inseparability of God and man: since the objective is 'to see God and the world in their unity, in the light of the modern homogeneous scientific world picture, without dissolving the difference in their unity' (DG 185). The assertion of some difference does not remove the essential homogeneity of both realities. The statements 'God is in this world and this world is in God', and 'God is the absolute who includes and creates relativity' (DG 185) are to be understood as implying this homogeneity. Taking the words at their face value they must mean that God has in himself an essential relationship to the world. It is true that the statement that God 'creates' this relationship seems once again to indicate that on his part it has been freely established. But since a relationship cannot properly be 'created', this can only be a metaphor and can only be understood as the practical embodiment of a relationship already existing in God.

With all this the author is aiming at a 'modern, dynamic understanding of God' (DG 188), an understanding which does not remove the fundamental unity of God and history, although it assigns to God a 'power over history'. It is true that in a new precautionary statement he wants God's historicity to be understood only 'analogously' (DG 188); but his statements about God's relationship to the world are meant in the proper sense. So, for example, he can say that 'God is oriented to the world: there is not a God without the world! And the world is totally related to God; there is not a world without God' (DG 672). The second sentence is correct – on the presupposition that God freely created the world. But the first, which is in no way meant analogically, means that God cannot exist without the world.

In harmony with this is the declaration that God's attributes can only be understood as 'active qualities for man and the world', and still more unambiguously, they are 'what God is, not in himself or from himself, but for man and the world, how he acts on man and the world' (DG 671). That God belongs to the world process and gains from it is shown by the statement: 'If God is really the infinite primal ground, primal support and primal meaning of the world and of man, it is clear that God loses nothing when man gains, but that God gains in so far as man gains' (DG 649).

This modern 'dynamic' picture of God has the characteristic marks of an evolutionary pantheism or panentheism which clearly contradicts the teaching of the Church (particularly Vatican I: DS 3001).

Since Küng does not recognise any supernatural order and reality (and hardly speaks of 'grace' other than in the sense of 'extrinsic grace'), the reasons for accepting the mystery of the Trinity are taken away. It is, therefore, not surprising that (in spite of the refutation, already made by the historians of dogma, of similar statements in *On being a Christian*) he criticises belief in the Trinity derived from 'hellenistic ideas' and 'the resultant dogmatic formulations' (DG 701). His reservations appear first in his ambiguous declaration that this truth 'is stressed by some as the central mystery of Christianity and is rejected by others as hellenistic speculation' (DG 699). Thus the impression is given that this belief is no longer firmly held in the Church. The author now pleads for a new interpretation of this doctrine which he says has become unintelligible. How he does this is shown by his interpretation of the words of Stephen (Acts 7:55ff). Stephen is said to have seen 'quite in the manner of Old Testament' (DG 700) only the 'glory' of God and the man Jesus by his side. The Holy Spirit on the other hand was in Stephen. He does not belong to the immanent Trinity but is only a power of God, which, with a view to the salvific work of Jesus, is brought into the world, and which again can also be regarded as identical with the life-giving power of the exalted Jesus.

Taken strictly, this changed interpretation of the Trinity means this: the 'Trinity' consists of 'God' (for whom the name Father is used in *On being a Christian* only with reluctance); the man Jesus exalted by the cross; and the power of the Spirit which comes from both. In the 'Trinity' it is only 'in the last resort a question ... of the one action of God himself' (DG 701). 'It is important to see the *unity* of Father, Son and Spirit as *revelation event and revelation unity*'. To be sure, 'what really matters is ... not to cancel the diversity of the "roles" of Father, Son and Spirit': but this concession to the teaching of the Church only makes the erroneousness of this interpretation clearer: the Trinity is only a matter of division of 'roles' in the history of salvation: this is a renewal of the false doctrine of sabellianism. What is left is only an 'apparent Trinity', which is basically only intended as a description of a somewhat differentiated relationship of God (understood as the fundamental dynamism of history) to the world.

It seems we must conclude: Küng does not admit the existence of a binding belief in a trinitarian God, and is unable to understand the meaning of this mystery. This is also clear from his statement that this belief – if it is kept at all – is 'anything but specifically Christian' (Chr 473). Here is a failure to understand that a purely unitary and solitary God would be a Being unfulfilled in himself, and dependent on the world. Küng does not realise that it is precisely the mystery of the Trinity which preserves the unique character of God's turning to and love for the world in Jesus Christ: for, if this love did not issue from the fulness of the relationships of persons sharing in the same nature, it would be due either to God's need for a human 'Thou' or to mere arbitrary decision. Consequently, it is a conviction of faith, not to be surrendered, that the mystery of the Trinity, which involves an immanent trinity in unity, is precisely what is specifically Christian. Here Küng could learn a lesson from Karl Barth, and reflect on what he says: 'it is the doctrine of the Trinity which essentially distinguishes as Christian the Christian teaching about God, and distinguishes the Christian concept of revelation from all other doctrine about God and all other concepts of revelation'.

Here one must recognise that it is not enough to describe the *appearances* of God as trinitarian. Much more, Christian faith is convinced that God is essentially a trinity. If anyone denies this belief or dismisses it as hellenistic speculation, or holds the view that it must of course be taken seriously as a historical fact but does not any longer regard it as important for today, he is tearing up the whole context of the Christian faith. Quite apart from the serious errors in his historical account of trinitarian doctrine, it would be already possible at this point to say that Küng's book disfigures and distorts the Christian and Catholic faith. It is, in fact, not too much to say that Küng's review of Christian trinitarian belief comes close to the attitude of rigid Jewish and Mohammendan monotheism.

54

Understandably this must have a negative effect on all other Christian truths about salvation. The fact that in *On being a Christian* the doctrine of creation is missing from this 'summa' of Christian faith could seem perhaps to be only a superficial deficiency, which is compensated for by occasional references to the 'Creator God'. But the reader who looks more deeply into Küng's theology will see clearly that this deficiency is also due to loss of faith in the Trinity: since a rigidly unitarian God cannot properly be thought of without any relationship to the world. Against the background of an unitarian concept, the creation is not a mystery and therefore need not be mentioned. But the omission of it here is an error which leads necessarily to a false definition of the purpose of creation. According to this book, the 'purpose of God's dealing with the world is always nothing more than man's well-being'. 'God wills nothing for himself, nothing for his own advantage, for his greater glory' (Chr 251), and this 'advantage' is in no way distinguished from a merely immanent and hedonistic striving for happiness. With such statements, recurring constantly in different forms, the Christian truth is reduced by half. In its fulness, it recognises that God has created man for his own (divine) glory, and that for this reason the final end of creation is the glory of God.

But it is an open question if worship and prayer are at all possible towards a God of the kind who cannot exist without the world. It is logical, therefore, that in *On being a Christian* Küng criticises the Catholic sacrifice of the Mass (Chr 426). His failure to discuss prayer is due, he says to 'the policy of the Roman Inquisition' which robbed him of the time needed for working out this line of thought (Chr 686f). However, given the picture of God in *On being a Christian*, one does not feel this as an omission. Characteristically, there is also no reference to prayer in *Does God exist?*, which was intended to supplement *On being a Christian*. The deficiency is not compensated for by his brief remark that 'we can speak to God', and that this is of decisive importance for prayer (DG 634). But this importance is nowhere demonstrated, especially as the truth of God's providence is eliminated: since 'the history of the world and of mankind does not proceed according to a preconceived, fixed plan' (DG 651). History is in fact only 'God's playing with and on the world' . . . a game for 'which he has laid down from the outset nothing but the rules' (DG 652) and in which man is a 'free partner' (DG 652). One cannot pray in any proper sense of the word to such a God; above all one cannot address a prayer of petition to a 'primal origin', 'primal support' and 'primary end', even though in the fashion of modern philosophers one 'can sing and dance before him' (DG 666). A non-Christian critic remarked laconically about this picture of God: 'If a modern understanding of God can be reached only in this way, then one has every reason to prefer older ideas and to go back beyond Hegel'.[96]

5

'JESUANISM' INSTEAD OF
BELIEF IN CHRIST

Where belief in a trinitarian God is wavering, it is difficult to erect a true belief in Christ, since the mystery of Christ grows out of the mystery of the Trinity. It is on the mystery of the Trinity, above all, that the truth of the 'pre-existence' of Christ, of his existence 'before time', is founded. This concept is 'difficult . . . for us today to conceive', since 'we can no longer accept the mythical ideas of that age, about a being descended from God, existing before time and beyond this world in a heavenly state; a "story of Gods" in which two (or even three) divine beings are involved' (Chr 446). The concept of pre-existence can, therefore, only mean that the relationship between God and Jesus 'did not emerge only at a later stage and — as it were — by chance, but existed from the beginning and has its foundation in God himself' (Chr 446). But of what man and his relationship to God could not exactly the same be said?

After this beginning, naturally, the mystery of the God-man can no longer be taken seriously. Küng indeed quotes the early Christian councils once more, but he stresses that the problem is much deeper: 'Chalcedon had by no means solved the problem permanently' (Chr 131) — as if mysteries of faith could be 'solved'. Yet Küng offers a simple solution. It is this: Jesus is ('in a deeply intimate-existential sense') a 'personal ambassador, trustee, confidant, friend of God' (Chr 317). Since this description seems, even to him, to be inadequate, he tries in many places to make it more adequate by using a series of superlatives. Thus Jesus is 'decisive', 'definitive', 'archetypal' for man (Chr 123); or he is God's deputy in 'uniqueness, underivability, unsurpassability' (Chr 449).

But the thinking Christian will dig deeper and ask: On what ground are the uniqueness and underivability of the phenomenon Jesus Christ based? They cannot be founded on the real divinity of Jesus, since according to Küng's theology that would mean going back to the myth of the 'two-God doctrine'. They must, therefore, be based on something human in Jesus, that is on the fact that Jesus 'was wholly and entirely man, with all the consequences of this' (Chr 449: but here his exemption from sin is not mentioned). More specifically, his uniqueness consists in this, that he is

56

not 'merely man, but true man' (Chr 449). It is here noticeable that Küng wants to ascribe a greater importance to the man Jesus by the choice of certain particularly strong expressions. But this increase in importance is not even verbally achieved: because what is the difference between 'mere' man and 'true' man? Is 'mere' man not 'true' man, and is 'true' man not also 'mere' man with all the human inferiority, which the author does not want to exclude and which causes him to say in one place that the originality of Jesus 'must not be exaggerated' (Chr 310). In other words, Küng does not succeed in demonstrating and proving theologically the uniqueness of Jesus. That cannot be done, if one no longer accepts as binding the faith of the Council of Chalcedon.

This also means that the decision made by Küng's theology to assert the exceptional character of a man Jesus of Nazareth turns out in the end to be just as unfounded and irrational as the decision to believe in God. His theology cannot explain why one's trust in God must be expressed precisely through the man Jesus of Nazareth. His explanation, that the call made known in this man is of divine origin, clarifies nothing: many religious men and prophets have passed on a call of divine origin, without there being any obligation or even authorisation to adhere to them so absolutely. Here one can in fact pass a more rigorous judgment: absolute adherence to a man (even the 'truest' man) is a subtle form of the old ancestor cult, or of the modern star-cult, but cannot ever be justified as a religion. Fundamentally, the 'Christology' of this 'theological *summa*' does not go beyond the Mohammedan formula Küng praises – 'the one God and his prophet' (Chr 96).

One cannot fail to recognise that this picture of Jesus does not resemble the Christ of Catholic faith. Neither does it meet the faith in Christ of early Reformation thought. When a critical thinker and a believer (the book is· constantly demanding that one be critical) fulfils the first requirement of criticism, namely to make distinctions, he will not be able to regard this explanation of the man Jesus of Nazareth as supernatural faith in Christ, but will see it as natural 'Jesuanism'. Adhering to such a completely human Jesus does not in the final analysis require any faith. Faith is always and only concerned with an object which is mysterious and unfathomable by human thought, an object which remains mysterious, even after it has been revealed. Thus it can be seen that in *On being a Christian* the understanding of faith and of its acceptance evaporates. The 'belief in Jesus' recommended here is no longer the word of Christ which comes from revelation and the doctrine proclaimed by the Church, the word which calls for the obedience of faith, and which, surpassing all human capacity, enables mankind to gain, through grace, a share in the mystery of the triune God.

The 'belief in Jesus' which Küng means is a subjective response to a

Jesus figure as pictured by a modern man who is a committed humanist and who is idealistically striving to improve the world. This Jesus can also appeal to those mentioned at the beginning of the book as its intended readers — people who claim to be 'atheists, gnostics, agnostics and positivists' (Chr 19): but they need not abandon their atheism or agnosticism. He is just a Jesus who does not face one with making a decision, since his teaching is only something highly reasonable, and really not denied by anyone — the humanising of the world and the acquisition of a higher quality of life.

Even then it must be recognised that Küng's Jesus-figure does not fit his constantly repeated claim to modernity, if one understands modern to mean new, unheard-of previously, not existing heretofore. The face is that this picture of Jesus has been drawn often before in the course of church history. The first efforts in this direction are to be found in the idea of Christ formed by the formerly Jewish Ebionites. These denied the pre-existence of Christ and the virgin birth, and saw in Jesus merely God's great messenger, described by another name in this book as 'God's legal representative'. This example shows that the denial of the true divinity of Christ, with all its logical consequences, is not an achievement of modern times nor a result of critical thought or of modern understanding of the world. The alternative of unbelief or half-belief has always been present as an antithesis to supernatural faith in Christ.

It is true that this alternative has been more widely and firmly represented and defended in modern times, and since the Enlightenment. But when compared to the naturalistic idea of Jesus in the Enlightenment, the Jesus picture of this book shows no real originality. Its rejection of every statement about Christ's essential nature, and of every metaphysical discussion of the mystery of his person, was already a feature of Schleiemacher (+ 1834): he also abandoned the truths that Christ is the second Person of the Trinity, that he rose from the dead, that he will come again; all that was left was Christ as the model of God's indwelling and of sympathy for fellowmen. Essentially that is exactly what this book is saying about Christ as the perfect man. Yet, the Christ of Schleiermacher is also distinguished by his 'essential sinlessness', which in practice raises him above the standard of the common man, whereas sinlessness (although testified to in the Bible) is not part of the picture of Jesus in *On being a Christian*. At any rate it is never mentioned. In this regard the book lacks the religious depth of Schleiermacher's or A. Ritschl's picture of Christ. Ritschl (+ 1889) also saw in Jesus only a supreme example of moral conduct, but still did not wish to abandon the idea of 'Christ's divinity', although he saw in this only the expression of a particular religious esteem for Jesus as a moral figure.

In the picture of Jesus given in this book all these characteristics are taken over from the past and put forward more emphatically, so that it could be justly said that here is nothing more than the start of a pompous 'return to the nineteenth century'.[97] The fact that this copy of a picture, long smothered in dust, can be produced as modern is understandable given the readership Küng aims at: but it is not justifiable either in history or in theology.

Nevertheless, a reader who is impressed by this humanistic Jesus could object that after all there is in the book a series of statements which emphasise the distinctiveness, in fact the uniqueness and simply the 'divineness', of the phenomenon Jesus. For example, Küng says that 'Jesus of Nazareth as the Christ . . . [is] finally authoritative, decisive, archetypal' (Chr 174); this Jesus had 'a special experience of God', 'a most unusual intimacy with him' (Chr 317); Jesus was the call of God, in 'uniqueness, underivability and unsurpassability' (Chr 449). These statements about Jesus, apparently giving him the highest attributes, correspond to the descriptions of Jesus common in liberal theology as the ultimate Revealer, the last and decisive Word of the Father to mankind.

In view of these statements of the unique greatness of Jesus, which are certainly not insignificant, one might ask what makes them insufficient. The main objection to them is that they do not touch upon the mystery of Christ's person, that they in fact rob it of meaning: for it is one thing to say that Jesus is an unsurpassable word of God to mankind, and another to declare that he is the Word of God himself made 'man', the Logos of the Father within the Trinity who was made flesh (Jn 1:14). This last statement alone is the centre of Holy Scripture and the quintessence of the mystery of Christ. Here also the mature Christian should be allowed the capacity to distinguish, and be expected to discern that there are essential differences lying behind similar combinations of words and slight variations of expression, and that these differences are as enormous and profound as the difference between God and man, between Creator and creature. It is just this difference and this separating chasm which are bridged over and closed in the mystery of Christ's person, since in him God and man were and are united in the person of the Word. That is the belief of the Church in Jesus Christ as the early councils of the Church expressed it. In this they did nothing which did not fit in with, or which contradicted Holy Scripture, since this truth is found in it, and can be demonstrated from it, by one who interprets Scripture in the spirit of the Church.

If a modern Christian can no longer rise to the height of this faith, one should not say that this is a personal moral fault. At most he can be reproached with lack of ability to make distinctions, and with the intellectual weakness of his failure to recognise that the 'Word made flesh' and the 'God-man' of the faith of the Church mean something other than the 'unsurpassable man' or the 'unique advocate' of God. But it should be possible to convince him, purely by intellectual argument, that all these highflown verbal descriptions of Jesus Christ as 'true' and not 'mere' man (Chr 449), lead in fact into a vacuum, in which true faith in Christ has no support, and in which it must ultimately sink; since if one thinks further, the question inevitably arises: Why must Christ be the Father's ultimate and final word to mankind, and how can he be the unsurpassable, unique, final revealer, the closest, most trusted and most intimate friend of God? This book, and the concept of Jesus which is fundamental to it, can give no answer to this question, which is essential for reason and faith. It can only repeat constantly with a certain monotony: That is how it is! Jesus is God's last and highest word to men. Here the thinking makes no progress and is obviously marking time. The argument has as it were run aground on a mere assertion which cannot be proved.

If one wishes to loosen up this obvious intellectual log-jam one can only say: God has arranged it so that Jesus is the last and the highest in the line of prophets, men of God and friends of God; this line had to have an end and reach its peak sometime. But this is not a valid explanation for a thinking believer: it amounts to admitting that the line could continue, that there could be a still higher revealer and a 'truer' man than Jesus. That is to say, if one in principle insists on a distance separating God and the man Jesus, it is possible to conceive that every approach of these two 'greats' could be closer, more intimate and more intensive. But then comes a series of questions, fatal for Christian faith: Has God perhaps acted here purely positivistically, wilfully and arbitrarily, when he ended the line of prophets and intimates with Jesus of Nazareth? Above all, to the modern man, influenced by the concept of evolution, another question, just as sceptical, will occur: If Jesus is only relatively the highest revealer of God and only relatively the most perfect man (the thrust of this 'Jesuology' is in fact, towards this relative character of the phenomenon of Jesus), why could not in the course of human history, the exact duration of which we cannot determine (Teilhard de Chardin gave it nevertheless two million years more before it ends), a still higher revealer of God come, and a more perfect man, than Jesus of Nazareth was. Should we then adhere so decisively and exclusively to this Jesus? Would it not be better to wait and hope that a still higher revelation is imminent for mankind? The result of this would be an appreciation of Christ and Christianity as parts of the history of religion, regarding both indeed as being highly valuable religious phenomena, but not as something absolute, permanent and final.

Now a conclusive answer can be given to the question why it is not enough, while speaking of Jesus, to give him the highest human attributes and titles which bring him as close as possible to God. If he himself is not this God in the real meaning of the word (and this can be held by theology without any diminution at all of his humanity), then even the loftiest descriptions are superficial, unexclusive and capable of being surpassed. No longer could we testify with the epistle to the Hebrews: 'Christ yesterday, to-day and for all eternity' (Hebr 1:36). We would have to ask another question, as the Baptist did in the time of mankind's expectation and before the revelation of Christ: 'Are you he who is to come or must we await another?' (Mt 11:3). Without belief in the essential unity of Jesus Christ with God, in the divine person of the Son, belief in Christ is not only vague but unfulfilled and empty.

A thoughtful faith cannot in the long run remain on this level of a human 'advocate' of God. In fact, if you reason out this possibility to its ultimate logical conclusions, this would be merely a form of the old-time hero-cult. For this reason, it has been rightly pointed out that the title 'God's advocate', which this book gives to Jesus by preference, is profoundly rooted in mythology. Thus we have a mythological flower springing up in a modern setting! Indeed, to stay with a modern comparison, one might illustrate the deeper background in time and history of this concept of Jesus by saying: This is more than anything else a modern star-cult; modern man also (even when he is actualising his religious potentialities) needs his hero, his idols and 'divas', whom he can on the one hand look up to with a kind of longing, but with whom he also wants to identify himself, so as not to suffer from the impossibility of fulfilling his longing. But man cannot identify himself with a God-man and therefore he has no 'use' for him in his piety, which anyhow is directed towards usefulness here and now.

The real Christian, on the contrary, knows why his faith must be directed towards the divine mystery of the person of Jesus Christ, and why he must hold firmly to the divinity of Christ. Küng could give the impression that belief in the divinity of Jesus Christ, and the formulation of a doctrine about the mystery of Christ's person (a doctrine which discusses and answers the question 'Who is this?' with all the powers of reason illuminated by faith), was due to greco-hellenistic thinking which would have been interested in the physical or metaphysical conditions of the person of Jesus Christ, and would have 'postulated and deduced from above (his) divine sonship' (Chr 449), 'in the style of ancient festal inscriptions and festal forms of address' (Chr 450). Against this one must firstly say, in agreement with modern exegesis, that the early Christian councils did not need to deduce the divine sonship of Jesus, since it was already to be found in Holy Scripture. According to the Protestant exegete E. Käsemann, the 'divine Sonship (in the metaphysical sense) is obviously taken for granted in the New Testament'.[98] The Catholic exegete R. Schnackenburg says that 'the two natures doctrine, still undeveloped, is included' in the declarations of the Gospel of St John (especially Jn 1:14).[99]

This means that Christian thought has added nothing to the primitive Christian faith, nor has it added any philosophical ideas. Indeed, Christian thinkers, basing themselves on the facts of salvation and redemption, also had to recognise and believe in the divinity of Christ, since this truth was not fully explicit at the beginning.

Christian thought was most profoundly convinced that Jesus Christ, as true man, must have been true God as well, for the purpose of our redemption: since as true man (even the 'true man' as described in this book) he could not have redeemed us. The whole debate about the Christological formulations in the first general councils, which often seems so theoretical, was not concerned with abstract statements about his essence, but with ascertaining and safeguarding the redemption brought about by Christ. With a lively consciousness of faith, confronted with the problems of salvation, they knew that mankind could not have been redeemed by a 'true man', even if he had lived ever so near to God, and ever so intimately with him. Then as now, Christian thought about the salvation brought about in Christ was not content to say that 'God and man are truly involved in the history of Jesus Christ' (Chr 449). It was much more convinced that it is only when the man Jesus Christ is at the same time true God, that he can redeem us; since redemption through a 'true man' would be only a refined form of self-redemption, such as mankind had continually attempted throughout the history of religion, and still attempts.

The results of research into the history of dogma (results tendentiously reported in this book) show that when the Greek theologians of the early councils (as asserted in Chr 448) devised the formulations laying down the unity of God and man (in Christ), they did not do this from necessity or because they had no other concepts to use. They could certainly have said such things as: Christ was very near to God; he was the man most intimately united to God, God was 'present' in him; but they knew that our redemption would be a non-event if the union of Jesus with God were not believed to be a unity of essence. Only this intrinsic reason could justify the 'imitation of Jesus' (Küng uses this expression in preference to redemption real and concrete). Apart from the fact that 'imitation' cannot redeem mankind, but instead presupposes redemption, it would be unjustified and irreligious, since here it would be the imitation of a man. If one wishes to give an intrinsic reason for the imitation of Christ, and not understand it as a mere offshoot of a covert hero-cult, one must answer the question 'Who is he?' with the faith of the Church: 'true man and true God!' Otherwise, one is imitating a religious dreamer.

The surrender of this truth logically produces noticeable effects on doctrine about the Church. The Church can no longer be understood as the 'body of Christ' but only as the 'community of those who have become in-volved in the cause of Jesus Christ' (Chr 478). The error goes further and ends in the complete failure to recognise a sacramental structure in the Church. Thus, the Eucharist is only a mere memorial and thanksgiving cele-bration: it is a 'sharing in the effect' (Chr 427) of Jesus's sacrifice of his life, but not the re-presentation of this sacrifice, and not the sacrifice of the Church as well as of the faithful. This community meal 'may be cele-brated as a joyous meal also for sinners' (Chr 427): which is in itself obvi-ous, unless behind this idea lies the demand made by Evangelical theo-logians that people in the state of sin (and without having received the sacrament of Penance, a sacrament not mentioned in this book) should be admitted to the Eucharist.

One must ask, in conclusion, if *Does God exist?* has in any respect cor-rected or withdrawn this humanistic Jesuanism, or has made a start towards the recognition of the real divinity of Christ and of the mystery of the God-man. This seems unlikely even from the start, if one takes seriously the author's own conviction that both books 'merge smoothly one into the other' (DG *xxiii*), and that they complement and illuminate each other (DG 566); at the beginning of *Does God exist?* Küng expressly says that in its final section repetitions of the theses of *On being a Christian* must be expected (DG *xxiii*).

So all the well-known statements turn up again: Jesus 'was the manda-tory, plenipotentiary, advocate, spokesman, advocate ... deputy of God' (DG 683). But in fact Jesus was not God's deputy: the consubstantial Son cannot be described as the Father's deputy but must be recognised as the God-man in person. Nor is this erroneous description corrected by calling Jesus a deputy of God who cannot be reached or surpassed (DG 683). The 'unsurpassability' remains here an assertion in words without meaning, since it is not based on Christ's divinity.

Someone might ask if Küng's erroneous Christological statements are not corrected by his occasionally granting Jesus the title 'Son of God'. But it must be noticed in what sense he uses this; it means only that Jesus is fulfilling a commission and a function for God: 'God himself encounters us in a unique and definitive way in the activity and person of Jesus' (DG 686) (and undoubtedly for Küng in the *human* person). This title expresses Jesus' 'significance as God's revealer' (DG 686). But to reduce Jesus – as here – to being one of the prophets does not adequately explain the mystery of his person. This is shown by Küng's speaking of Jesus as only one of God's sons, distinguished from the others only through the cross. 'It is the cross that distinguishes Jesus from other "sons of God"' (DG 689). Now, it is quite impossible to understand how even the most self-sacrificing death could transform a human being into a son of God, (in fact, no being can 'become' God), unless this sonship be understood as purely moral and functional, and therefore distinguished only in degree from the sonship of other human beings. In fact, it seems impossible to reconcile such a 'sonship' of Jesus with the mystery of Christ's real divinity, and of the hypostatic union of his human nature with the true Son of God.

This is clear also from Küng's definition of 'incarnation', which seems to amount to a denial of this mystery: 'God's becoming man in Jesus means that in all Jesus' talk, in his whole proclamation, behaviour and fate, God's word and will have assumed a human form. . . . He is . . . , in human form, God's Word, will, Son' (DG 685). Here too it becomes clear that, apart from the almost Docetic concept of an apparent 'human form' of Jesus, the word 'Son' is used asn an equivalent of 'God's will'. An incarnation of this kind could be attributed to every prophet and every religious figure of mankind. Naturally, this involves also the denial — en passant — of the pre-existence of Christ (DG 684) and the miraculous birth of Jesus (DG 689).

Yet, is not Küng's acceptance of the Nicene formulation that Jesus Christ is 'God from God, Light from Light, true God from true God, begotten, not made, of one Being with the Father' (DG 685) to be regarded as a return to the belief of the Church? When he appeals to the early councils of the Church, one must constantly remember the fundamental principle he repeatedly lays down: that he accepts, for example, the Council of Chalcedon, but that 'for me everything depends on the correct understanding of this'.[100] Here again appears the demand that one should embrace only an *interpretation* of the faith, and this interpretation is determined by Küng himself.

If his attempts to link up with the early councils of the Church are read in the light of this reservation, it will be seen that they do not reproduce the faith of the Church, but rather his interpretation of it, an interpretation which is actually a misrepresentation. This can be easily recognised in the context, if one bears in mind the pre-condition he lays down that, in relation to Christ, the statements about his function are to receive prime attention, and that all statements about him must be viewed in 'historical perspective' (DG 685). We find here also that Jesus 'is the revelation of God's power and wisdom'. Corresponding to this is the assertion that the fourth Gospel describes Jesus, the word of God, only 'indirectly as equal to God'. Thus the acceptance of the Nicene formulation must also be understood only 'indirectly'; 'directly' Jesus is and remains the prophet of God, who carried out God's will. So also the formulation of the Council of Chalcedon is given the completely misleading interpretation that 'in the story of Jesus Christ God and man are truly involved' (DG 687). In the history of what man does this not happen literally?

So the authentic teaching of the Church is not reached when the author reproduces the meaning of the Nicene formulation and adds the explanation 'God (was) in Jesus Christ' (DG 685). God's presence in or dwelling in a man does not at all mean a personal union with God, or the consubstantiality of two divine persons. Moreover, this fundamentally Nestorian formulation has been rejected by the Council of Ephesus (DS 256). Thus the conclusion is completely justified, that Küng's appeal to the early Christian councils is the product of a process of muddled thinking which in practice tends to lead people astray.

6

THE EMPTIED CROSS
AND FALSIFIED
RESURRECTION

Although *On being a Christian* and *Does God exist?* say that Jesus of Nazareth is the standard for deciding what is Christian, they are still not able to reach and recognise in this Jesus the mystery of his divinity. Obviously, they cannot therefore be satisfied with describing Jesus as the 'advocate, deputy and representative of God' (DG 688) in order to identify what is specifically Christian and unique about him. Thus already in *On being a Christian* Küng names the 'ultimate distinctive feature of Christianity': the cross of Christ and Christ as the crucified one (Chr 410). As a further explanation *Does God exist?* adds: 'It is not the fact that Jesus of Nazareth was a Son of God which distinguished him at that time from so many heroes and demigods, who were also sons of God', but 'it is the cross that distinguishes him from other "sons of God"' (DG 688f). (This is an admission that for him Jesus was only one of many sons of God.)

Now it is an essential truth of the Christian doctrine of the redemption that the God-man has ascended the cross and has redeemed us through it (and through his resurrection from the dead). Christian belief about the redemption has held firmly not only to the mystery of the divine person Jesus Christ, but also to his sacrifice on the cross and his resurrection. This unique person and what he accomplished on the cross are essential features of the complete Christian belief in the redemption.

But this belief has never accepted and professed that the cross distinguished Jesus from other sons of God. Such a statement logically involves the assertion that it was through the cross that Jesus became the Son of God. In this way the crucifixion seems to acquire a particular significance: it gives Jesus for the first time a decisive divinity. But there the question arises: What significance can the crucifixion have if it is a crucifixion endured, not by the God-man, but by an 'advocate' of God, in whose life God himself was at work? Such a crucifixion cannot, in fact, be understood as a real, objective and actual redemption, as the Christian faith holds. The omission of the divinity of Jesus deprives the crucifixion of its significance. Thus it must be said: the cross can never make Jesus 'the only-begotten

Son of God'; it derives its significance only from the God-man. But where there is no belief in the mystery of the God-man, the cross loses its importance, and Christianity becomes a failure as a religion of redemption.

On being a Christian also comes close to emptying the cross. On the basis of an ingenious but false identification of the Anselmian satisfaction theory with the teaching of the Church — a teaching which already at the time of the Council of Ephesus spoke of the 'expiatory sacrifice of Jesus for us' (DS 261) — the book comes not only to reject the concept of sacrifice, but to abandon the truth of the wiping out of sins: since 'suffering, death, concupiscence, sin do not disappear' (Chr 423) and therefore 'what should be most prominent in the "for us" are not sins but . . . men' (Chr 426). All men are called to believe by the death on the cross (426). Its effectiveness lies in the 'example' of Jesus which 'lives on in our memory'. That is the old Pelagian doctrine about the life and death of Jesus, a doctrine which does not see them as objectively effecting salvation, but in fact only as an example. Moreover, Jesus' death cannot attain any profound ontological depth since he did not attach any meaning to his dying. This assertion is made in a veiled manner: 'We still do not know exactly what he thought and felt as this death came upon him' (Chr 340). The words of Jesus during his Passion as given in the Gospels are simply ignored.

But this is not only a question of what Küng calls our defective knowledge. Since during this event the Father did not say a single word to Jesus (a remarkable contradiction of the intimacy with God otherwise so much emphasised, which obviously cannot be maintained), and since it was a God-less death, Jesus certainly cannot have thought about a redemption of mankind. On the basis of such presuppositions he can scarcely be considered the redeemer of mankind. Thus the death of Jesus, which Küng asserted to be the decisive and specific standard, is deprived of all that is specifically Christian, since the Nazarene is, once again, not needed as an example of total failure in which allegedly God remains his last support (but how does Küng suddenly claim to know this, and how can he speak as well of an absolute abandonment of Jesus by God?: Chr 341. It can be seen how clear thinking is lost in the course of this dialectical playing with words.) In the course of the world's history many other religious men have died, and we often know for certain that they suffered death as a sacrifice for others (take, for example, Maximilian Kolbe). Would it not be better then to keep to these instances of an exemplary human death? The manner in which the death of Jesus is described in the book is so lacking in every 'specifically Christian' factor, that the whole account practically amounts to an almost complete refutation of the author's thesis.

Neither is this minimalist conception of the cross and of the redemptive suffering of Jesus corrected in *Does God exist?* Where they are mentioned, Jesus is valued only as an example of the goodness of God, before whom one should not tremble: for Jesus reveals the 'friendly God', and in fact does this 'in his whole being and conduct, speaking and acting, also in his suffering and dying' (DG 686). Thus the whole purpose of Christ's suffering is to say to mankind: 'Where Jesus suffers and dies, there is God's hidden presence' (DG 686). Christ by his whole life and death is 'a model of being human' (DG 688), on which a man can trustingly rely. In another approach, the cross is spoken of in this way: 'The sign of shame is for him a sign of victory, of liberation and salvation, a call to abandon a life of selfishness' (DG 689). Even a brief analysis of this sentence, shows that it is only for Christ that the cross is said to be a sign of victory, and not for us; that it is regarded as a sign of redemption for him, although he did not need redemption. What is left for us, for mankind, is only the model for 'a life without fear . . . through struggle, suffering and death' (DG 689). One cannot find any statement here that the redemption has in principle taken sin away from men, and granted them the divine life, but even with the best of good will such a statement could find no place here. That the cross is only the intimation or strengthening of the presence of the good God, is not what the Christian message of redemption means.

In Küng's reference to the resurrection of Jesus the specifically Christian element also fails to appear. It must first be said that in all contexts in which he mentions 'death and resurrection' together, he puts emphasis on the death of Jesus and his exemplary significance for mankind, as a person whose trust in God has failed. This also is a characteristic of a line of thought which aims at humanism. Death and the cross are of course basic human experiences which can be thought of by every thoughtful man. Plato already knew that human life is marked by the cross and that the just man must suffer. Consequently, anyone who reminds man that his existence involves a deep level which is manifested in the cross, is doing something which is profoundly human, but still not specifically Christian. The theology of the cross (as such) is properly only an element of merely natural piety. The 'Christian possibility' properly so called, the 'specifically Christian feature', is rather the overcoming of the cross in a resurrection which is seen as being just as real, and which forms part of history. But here the train of thought becomes 'uncoupled'. Küng's declaration that the raising from the dead, the resurrection, are only metaphorical, not even analogous concepts (Chr 379), is revealing. Belief in the resurrection is therefore only a 'radicalizing of faith in God' (Chr 360). In it we have what is basically no more than a new version of the 'basic confidence' in God's faithfulness, the significance of which provides no certainty for the continued life of Christ or of mankind. A critical thinker will ask himself why, in view of the evidence justifying the fundamental trust in God so

stressed by the author, an additional sign of God's faithfulness is needed —
and moreover a sign which was in reality no sign; since the 'resurrection',
as interpreted by Küng, is in fact only a 'code word', an enigmatic expression indicating that Jesus is alive and with the Father. But of this one must
again say: that is the situation of every man who dies in grace and is await-
ing the resurrection.

This lack of any belief in a real and actual resurrection which brings salvation is largely the result of another circumstance, which today poses a
threat to the entire Christian and Catholic faith — the abandonment of any
real belief in miracles and the adoption of a frivolous playing with the
word 'miracle'. A miracle is no longer seen as an extraordinary action of
God's power, an action which produces effects in our real world, which
our world cannot produce of itself, but to which our world is open on
account of its relation to the Creator. Küng first uses in this connection a
misleading definition, describing miracles as 'interventions' by God in the
order of creation. Thus he surrenders them to the ridicule of scientific
thought. But even from a theological standpoint, with this incorrect description, belief in miracles is from the start incorrectly reduced to a deistic
concept of God, according to which God must intervene, as it were, 'from
outside' in his creation. (The theological formulation which Küng uses
here — 'violations of the laws of nature' — distorts once more the valid
theological definition of 'miracle'.)

Küng cannot recognise in the world any action of God which goes beyond the powers and laws of the immanent course of the world. God cannot suspend 'the laws of the system which he himself laid down' (DG
653). This statement, which must be taken as a theological argument, has
no meaning unless God is said to be identical with his creation and its laws,
or 'gets completely "involved" in what happens in the world' (DG 651).
For this reason, according to Küng the accounts of miracles are merely intended to indicate that God works together with the forces of nature —
not that he does anything which transcends these forces and the course of
the world. 'They proclaim not a God detached from the world and from
history, apathetically leaving the world to its fate, but a God who gets
completely "involved" in what happens in the world' (DG 651). Thus
God as the basis of the world remains in a stronger position, but this basis
is immanent in reality and is necessarily bound up with it, so that ultimately he can only work in harmony with this reality and with the laws by
which he himself and this reality are bound. By this denial of miracles
Küng again argues that God and the world are necessarily and essentially
correlated.

From this lack of belief in a realistic and salvific resurrection, there
arise consequences for belief in the final destiny of mankind.

That I am not reading too much into Küng's thinking on this subject is shown by his failure to speak clearly about the heavenly existence of the glorified Christ and his continuing activity, especially in the Church and the sacraments. The very notion of a coming of Christ in judgment (and not just the language used to describe that event) is expressly rejected as mythological. 'Better to speak of all men being gathered together in God' (Chr 394). It is not that Christ will come as judge; his death and his victory over death in a so-called 'life' are already the judgment. But what is meant here by judgment?: for in Küng's quite cursory treatment of eschatology, he considers as a serious possibility Origen's theory of universal reconciliation, and recommends everyone to await the final encounter with God 'in a spirit of joy and composure' (Chr 396). Should we not therefore give up the idea of judgment altogether, and preferably speak of an 'appearance of a judgment'? And finally what can 'being gathered together in God' mean, since from the very beginning, the understanding of God as a person is not clear, and the more or less transpersonal understanding of God, as in the oriental religions, is recommended (Chr 113)?

How wavering the goal he proposes for human life is, becomes clear from his call on us 'to transcend the present state of things, not in the sense of entering into a world beyond this, but in the sense of rising to that ultimate reality on which we can absolutely rely and which we call God' (Chr 447). Here God is not something special raised above reality (that would be supranaturalism) but simply identical with reality, into which every man must become merged, just as Jesus was merged; for it is no longer possible to speak of a personal existence of Christ together with the Father, as lord, supporter and judge of the world. And this is in a way logical: anyone who denies the pre-existence of the Son cannot easily accept his after-existence. Each truth conditions the other; they are two sides of one and the same mystery.

7

THE SURRENDER OF THE
MARIAN MYSTERY

The mystery of Christ loses meaning not least when it is deprived of the support and context of the Marian mystery: particularly through the teaching of Vatican II, Catholic Christians have become more conscious that the connection of Mary with the Church is a characteristic element of the faith and of piety, and has a reciprocal effect on the mystery of Christ. Evangelical theologians have again and again declared that the mystery of Mary is an integral part of the Catholic faith and develops its understanding of the mystery of the Church. Karl Barth's statement is well known: 'the Mother of God proclaimed in Roman Catholic dogma is the [basic] principle and essence of the Catholic concept of the Church'. The essential nature of the Church as the instrument under Christ of salvation, as receiver of salvation in virginal faith, and mediator of grace in fruitful motherhood, finds in Mary a radiant illustration, so that Mary sheds light on the Church and the Marian character of the Church becomes clear. 'So Mary and the Church are a single mother and yet two, one virgin and yet two' (Isaac of Stella). *On being a Christian* is not only not interested in this mystery, but directly and determinedly rejects it. Küng puts the virginal conception of Christ on the same level as the extraordinary events accompanying the birth of other founders of religions (Chr 437), and sees it as a symbol (or indeed a myth of Egyptian origin) for the 'divine sonship' of Jesus: but this title, in turn, is again only a symbol, a kind of mythological expression; thus, in one place (Chr 167) Joseph is expressly described as the father of Jesus in the natural sense of the word (Küng takes no notice of contrary findings of exegetical research).

Although his remarks about the divine motherhood are expressed more in the manner of a debate, the result is equally negative. How far away this is from the Catholic understanding of the faith, how much Küng has lost the ability to think theologically, is shown by his statement that 'God cannot be born' (Chr 460): it could as equally be put forward by a non-Christian philosopher of religion, who has had no contact with Catholic theology. It is a statement which is possible only after a denial of the incarnation of God. So one error dovetails with another.

On being a Christian takes no notice of the fact that the whole teaching of Vatican II about the Church culminates in the mystery of Mary. Since this mystery is denied, not only does Küng make the self-confident assertion that we can no longer venerate the Church as 'mother', but something more significant occurs: the Church loses its mystical dimension and the symbolic force of its existence as spouse and virgin. Quite in keeping with this book's whole approach, the Church becomes a machine under the control of theological engineers. Küng's ultimate objective was to make the Church more humane, but without acceptance of the mystery of Mary. Against this it must be asserted that 'without mariology the Church is in danger of imperceptibly becoming inhuman' (Hans Urs von Balthasar). One cannot meet this danger with the almost frivolous confession that 'the author too likes to celebrate Christmas, and sings "Silent night, holy night" without too many inhibitions' (Chr 127). Emotional delight of this type is no accident: there has always been a close connection between weakening in dogmatic belief, and pietistic sentimental devotion.

In *Does God exist?* the 'Christmas miracle' and the truth about Mary suffer the same rejection. Since 'there is no mention anywhere in the New Testament of the incarnation of God himself' (DG 684: in spite of Jn 1:14), no such event occurred; and therefore the birth of Christ cannot be identified as the point in time at which God became man. Incarnation is only a code word for the idea that God's word and will are expressed in Jesus, and this happened throughout his whole life (DG 185). Hence the demand that the incarnation should not be referred 'to the mathematical or mystical moment of the birth or conception of Jesus' (DG 685). This statement does not exclude, as a purely theoretical assumption, the possibility of such a 'mystical moment' at the beginning of the life of Jesus with which the mystery of Mary could be linked; yet no mention is made of the infancy narrative of Matthew and Luke: instead Küng asserts that for the recognition of the so-called 'Son of God' there is no need at all of 'mythological, semi-mythological and legendary embellishments' (DG 688). Thus, 'according to Mark, the divine sonship rests not on a miraculous birth or conception but on the mandate of God ... ' (DG 689). But no Catholic can doubt that this mystery is basically true, and that the mystery of the incarnation cannot be true if there is no mystery of Mary's virginal motherhood of Christ.

8

THE RENEWED DENIAL OF INFALLIBILITY

In the decisive books *On being a Christian* and *Does God exist?*, which I have selected for the purpose of discerning Küng's doctrinal views, the error, frequently maintained, about the infallibility of the Church and the pope is not exactly the most prominent, although it is not entirely absent. In *On being a Christian* (19), for example, we find the declaration that the author, 'unimpressed by ecclesiastical doctrinal constraints', wants to proclaim the truth as he sees it, and that '"truths", articles of faith, dogmas are ... so difficult to understand and to assimilate' (Chr 411). (In *Does God exist?* he complains that, even today, the Church one-sidedly emphasises the continuity and identity of its proclamation and 'up to our times the infallibility of its teaching': DG 111.) Such statements show that he is unwilling to withdraw any of his assertions about the infallible teaching of the Church, which were censured earlier.

This circumstance appears all the more remarkable since in a letter to the Congregation for the Doctrine of the Faith (4 September 1974) he made the concession that he would review his doctrinal opinions, and would not wish to exclude the possibility 'that in the course of time my doctrinal position could be assimilated to that of the magisterium'.[101] This was the particular circumstance that moved the Congregation, in a declaration of 15 February 1975, not to withdraw his *missio canonica*, but to warn him not to repeat his erroneous theses about the magisterium and the infallibility of the Church. The fact that the Congregation acted in such a restrained way led the President of the German Episcopal Conference soon afterwards to declare that obvious progress had been made.[102] However, in a manner calculated immediately to lessen the importance of the Congregation's statement, Küng referred to a 'truce laboriously arrived at'.[103] This interpretation is a good illustration of his characteristic style of judgment and interpretation. Later he declared, at the Stuttgart Colloquium of January 1977, that it had been a 'compromise' to which he had remained 'very faithful'.[104] Although the words 'truce' and a 'compromise' corresponded to the true meaning of the Roman document less than they showed Küng's art in interpretation, he did still agree that he had accepted an obligation of restraint in regard to the theses against infallibility. At the same time he remarked, with an obvious air of superiority, that not a single theologian had even once expressed criticism of the omnibus volume[105] in which he took stock of the infallibility debate.[106] That is in fact demonstrably false[107], but shows up his unshakable self-assurance.

In view of the fact that he had himself spoken of a 'truce', a 'compromise', and once actually of a 'proposal for an armistice'[108] to the Congregation, in February 1979, he suddenly caused surprise by declaring, in a preface to A. B. Hasler's *How the Pope became infallible*, that he had always emphasised his 'continual readiness for a discussion' but 'without compromise on the matter at issue'.[109] To make things clear he added: 'but an armistice agreement in so fundamental a question cannot be concluded, and has also never been concluded'.[110] The question may be left with the critical reader as to what to make of such self-contradiction.

At any rate the Congregation was quite entitled to declare in its statement of 15 December 1979 that the author had 'to date in no way changed those views of his already mentioned' and that 'he had put his concept forward still more expressly'[111] in Hasler's book.

A perusal of the preface to Hasler shows in fact that here, in a very short space, and with extreme force, the dogma of the infallibility of the Church and of the Pope is denied, and flatly declared to be false; he calls for its withdrawal. In Küng's view, the arguments of Hasler prove the need to revise the decisions of the first Vatican Council. This would give to the Catholic Church and Catholic theology, and also to the whole of Christendom a way out of a situation which has become untenable, into a new future'.[112] Leaving aside his criticism of the particular dogma, this assertion proves that this Catholic theologian no longer recognises the doctrine of the Church that articles of faith solemnly proclaimed by the Church are essentially irreformable. When he speaks in this context of a situation which has become untenable, one may be permitted to remark that, properly speaking, it is only for himself that this situation has become untenable.

Judged from a purely formal standpoint, it is firstly remarkable into what company he brings this charism of infallibility, which was granted by God to the Church, and which has a significant role in the theology of salvation. He compares it with the infallibility claimed by kings and emperors and latterly by dictators, and again, covering the perversity of such comparisons in the seemingly harmless form of a question, he goes on: 'Criticism of the infallibility of parties who are always "in the right" and of their modern successors has been and still is — from Moscow to Havana — stamped out by every possible oppressive and repressive method. And (many people ask) what about the infallibility of churches that are always ' 'in the right"? of their previous and present representatives who appeal to the Holy Spirit?'[113]

Without offering any evidence about who or how numerous these 'many' people are (or if they are not, possibly, marginal groups who have played up this problem in recent years) Küng supplies himself with the answer to these sham questions (an answer which he again presents as a decision passed by a newly established kind of general consent). He demands that the 'demythologisation of the absolute and authoritatian magisterium which started with John XXIII and the Second Vatican Council [which itself took up the infallibility doctrine of the First Vatican Council, and proclaimed it again] 'should be carried to a conclusion, replacing the magisterium by a genuine spiritual authority, so that the Church might be freed from all the arrogance, compulsion, and indeed dishonesty of curialist theology and administration'.[114] With these and similar sentences, he is calling for the surrender of this article of faith.

Since he refers here to 'dishonesty', and at the same time appeals to the model put forward by Vatican II, the counter-question can well be asked: Where, in fact, is his honesty, if he suppresses sentences like these from Vatican II: 'The holy Synod once more proposes for the firm belief of all the faithful this teaching about the institution, permanence, power and import of the sacred primacy which belongs to the Bishop of Rome and his infallible magisterium' (*Lumen Gentium* 18), and 'the individual bishops do not indeed possess the prerogative of infallibility; however, when separated throughout the world but maintaining the bond of communion with each other and with the successor of Peter, they teach authentically matters of faith and morals and unanimously teach a particular doctrine as finally binding, then they proclaim infallibly the teaching of Christ' (ibid. 25). In view of the fact that Küng does not shrink from reproaching this dogma of faith with 'compulsion', 'arrogance' and 'dishonesty' (a manner of speaking without parallel in the language of the Church), one cannot refrain from asking if those uninhibited attacks, and particularly the accusation of 'dishonesty', do not in all strictness recoil back upon himself.

This is confirmed by the way in which he describes for his readers the meaning and content of the dogma of infallibility. His object is to suggest to them the intrinsic impossibility and misleading nature of this truth of faith. Thus, for example, in what is simply a question of fact, he slips in a false interpretation: Pope John XXIII, he says, when he decided not to look for definitions in Vatican II, really wanted to surrender the claim to papal infallibility. 'Again and again he had stressed in very different ways his own humanness, limitations, indeed now and again his fallibility. He had no aura of infallibility'.[115] Pius XII, on the contrary, because of the dogma of the bodily assumption of Mary into heaven, which Küng describes as 'disputed' and 'uncertain', is accused of having unnecessarily made use in his private capacity of a dubious supreme authority: 'There was one Pope who, not quite one hundred years after Vatican I, thought that finally he must make use of the fulness of power ascribed to the Pope by the Council but never used, in order to proclaim an infallible definition of doctrine.'[116] In both cases the impression is given that 'infallibility' was a personal 'ambition' (the expression is used in connection with John XXIII) which one pope had renounced and which the other refused to renounce, thus damaging the Church. Here at the beginning the attitudes of both popes to a truth of faith, attitudes which are questions of historical fact, are falsely described. (one could even say that John XXIII is branded here as a scorner of a defined Church doctrine.)

This falsification of the historical figures of two popes leads on to a completely wrong description of the meaning of this dogma. There is no mention of the fact that infallibility belongs firstly to the whole Church, and that it is shared in a particular manner by the whole people of God: according to Vatican II (from which the Church has, according to Küng, in his first statement after the decision of 18 December 1979, allegedly departed) 'the whole body of the faithful, who have an anointing that comes from the Holy Spirit, cannot err in matters of belief' (*Lumen Gentium* 12). The author's whole description of this dogma gives the impression that the pope, completely apart from the Church (as is alleged particularly about Pius XII) is defending 'a personal claim to domination and power'[117] in order to be able to justify 'all the denunciations and dismissals, sanctions and excommunications, all the methods of manipulation and repression, threats and spying, used by the Curia and the nuncios.'[118]

Thus, he mistakes the proper content of papal infallibility when he says that this dogma 'protects and renders secure numberless doctrines and practices'[119] of the Church, where in fact it refers only to the proclamation of a teaching of faith and morals by an act which is definitive and is subject to quite definite conditions and presuppositions (*Lumen Gentium* 25). It is therefore false and tendentious to say, as he does, that 'infallibility belongs to the curialist system more than to the Catholic Church as it has understood itself to be from the beginning.'[119]

If Küng had researched, in a proper historical way, this understanding of itself possessed by the Church from the beginning, he would have discovered sufficient proofs of the existence of the 'matter' of 'infallibility' of the Church and of the pope.[121] This spiritual gift granted to the Church basically means that the truth of Jesus Christ, contained in his Church, continues still, and can be expressed, with the help of the Holy Spirit, in words which assert and rightly lay claim to being the truth. 'Infallibility' (as understood in the Catholic Church, whose faith on this point Küng evidently no longer shares, since he regards it as a curialist usurpation) is the gift granted to the Church through the power of the eschatological event of the incarnation and of its continued operation in the Holy Spirit — the gift of being able to declare without error the teaching of Christ in a decisive case. Infallibility is a necessity to serve the word of God, which otherwise would be at the mercy of a personal gift of the Spirit (as in the *internum testimonium Spiritus Sancti* in the Reformation concept) or would fall under the control of arbitrary interpretation by individuals, as Küng himself ceaselessly demonstrates.

No protection from this kind of arbitrary interpretation is provided by the historical-critical method, again and again emphasised by Küng. He would like to use this method to lay claim to modern scientific expertise before a semi-scientific public. Anyone slightly more informed about the subject will assert that the author does not know, or takes no account of, the discussion going on to-day in theological circles about the limits of historical-critical method. If he did, he would have to come to terms with the fact that this method 'was always only partially usable for historical tradition'[122], since tradition and the so-called 'operating history' of historical testimonies do not enter into its limited field of view. But it is precisely the neglect of tradition as obligatory in matters of faith, that is a characteristic mark of Küng's method. He thinks he can dismiss a truth of faith like infallibility with the statement that 'in the New Testament and in the first three centuries' there is no support 'for an infallibility of Peter'.[123] He does not see that in general no truth of supernatural faith can be comprehended by the methods of critical history alone. This method, especially as used today in uncritical combination with the criterion of 'acceptability to contemporary man', is 'no longer in a position to think concretely about God's action in history, to take seriously the ecclesiological connection of all consequential biblical tradition, or to distinguish properly between the knowledge derived from scientific history, which is in principle subject to revision, and the knowledge of faith, which gives certainty.'[124]

In Küng it is always a question of the same false conclusion: just as he cannot prove the divinity of Christ from Scripture, by using the tools of the positivist historian, so he cannot recognise in Scripture the infallibility of the Church in its beginnings (cf. particularly 1 Tim 3:15). That is, in fact, not possible with the help of a positivist and immanentist method, which obviously cannot catch anything supernatural in its coarse net. Küng fails fundamentally to recognise the theological principle that Holy Scripture is a book of the Church and can only be rightly read and understood in the living tradition of the Church.

Since he does not recognise this principle, and does not take serious account in his theological principles of the special character of theology as a scientific analysis of the faith, an analysis carried out within the Church, it was possible for him, in the course of the controversy about infallibility, to produce this inaccurate statement: 'Not a single theologian nor a single official tribunal have, up to now, been able to produce any proof that articles of faith (and tribunals standing behind them) can be guaranteed infallible by the Holy Spirit'[125], but in fact all Küng's logical and historical errors about this article of faith have been identified. Moreover, this statement reveals once more a profound ignorance of what Catholic teaching is about: firstly, there is of course no such thing as a logical (rational) proof of a mystery of faith; and secondly, one can only propose arguments to someone if he accepts the basic principles of the problem under discussion (for example, one can carry on a logical discussion only with a person who accepts the principles and rules of logic). But as the controversy over infallibility has shown, Küng no longer accepts the principles governing the handing on of the Catholic faith. Obviously, then, he cannot any longer allow himself to be convinced by the assertion of these principles. This inability on his part is not a proof that he has triumphed in this debate; but he thinks he has, because he goes so far as to say: 'But excommunication, suspension, withdrawal of authority to teach have not happened in the new infallibility debate and are unlikely to occur in the future.'[126]

As regards the foundations of Küng's position, which he claims to be indubitable, any objective observer who can appreciate a theological proof must see that they have been refuted. Thus, it could be demonstrated that there is a logical contradiction in the statement he repeats in his preface to Hasler: 'The Church remains established in the truth in spite of all its errors': it lies, of course, in the assertion that 'statements can be true and false' at the same time.[127]

This assertion goes against the principle of contradiction, according to which the same thing can never be positively asserted and denied simultaneously, that is, cannot be regarded as simultaneously true and false. O. Semmelroth discloses the violation of this first principle of every orderly thinking, when he declares: 'For him [Küng] every statement is simultaneously true and false. There can therefore be no infallible statement at all about reality, especially about God.'[128]

This would mean that truth and error could no longer be distinguished in the Church, which is the teacher of truth. The Church would foster an error in faith just as much as a truth of faith. It would be able to offer to men nothing more than a mixture of truth and error.

Küng cannot escape these negative consequences by making 'the situation' the proper 'criterion of truth'[129] and by bringing in pragmatism as a rule for determining truth, as he put it in a previous statement: 'A good practical result, which fits the real situation, can in certain circumstances make a statement, "in itself" false, to be true: a bad result which does not suit the situation can in certain circumstances turn into an error a statement which "in itself" is true'.[130] This is a relativistic and pragmatic attitude to the problem of truth which makes the validity of truth dependent on its being adapted to practical needs and ultimately dependent on the majority opinion of individuals or experts. In this case, those Evangelical 'German Christians' who most decidedly conformed to the situation during the Nazi period would 'in spite of their many mistakes' have been doing 'the right thing', 'the true thing'.

It will be seen that with basic principles of this sort, a unitary, permanent and binding confession of faith can no longer be maintained in the Church. Against this, the philosopher H.E. Hengstenberg and others have shown, that 'on the level of human reason, there are timelessly valid truths, which can claim permanent validity as far as their intrinsic meaning is concerned':[131] something which the Church claims and establishes with heightened meaning on the level of the truth of faith (DS 3020).

Küng, in the preface to Hasler, makes the further criticism that a faith handed down by an infallible Church would give 'the faithful a superhuman security and safety' which 'would allow them to forget all fear of human uncertainty, freedom and the venture which faith involves:'[132] here also he fails to understand the nature of faith: for the infallibility of the Church does not in any way replace the freedom of the act of faith, nor does it deprive a man of the need to make a decision in face of the challenge of the mystery of faith. Rather, it merely provides the condition for a humanly responsible faith, which has been passed on since the time of the Apostles through unerring witnesses of the truth, and which is kindled through their unerring witness. Otherwise we should have to be supported in the transmission of the faith by the ever changing findings of historical research and its interpreters, who are continually liable to error. But faith does not come from a fallible scholarship.

In all Küng's assertions about the charism of infallibility, granted to the Church for the decisive validation of the truth of the faith, it can be seen that he does not any longer recognise this fundamental principle of Catholic teaching and faith. It is not remarkable that a highly intelligent theological writer can, by a process of sheer conjecture, arrive at different theories; but what is surprising is his intellectual failure to distinguish this position from that of the Catholic Church. Whereas one cannot reproach the Church, which possesses this ability to distinguish, for making practical use of it. If it did not, it would be untrue to itself.

9

CORRECTION OF COURSE:
IN WHAT DIRECTION?

The 'radical correction of course' of the Christian faith and of the Church which Küng keeps calling for in *Does God exist?* is an incontrovertible fact' in view of the evidence I have given. It would be an injustice to him if this objective of his were not taken seriously; but one is therefore also justified in charging him with the full gravity of the consequences of this 'course correction'.

These consequences are indeed grave, and go far beyond mere details. As he repeatedly declares, the Christian faith and the Church in their entirety must be subjected to radical change. Yet he refuses to allow interpreters and critics to reproach him, except for certain failings in balance and occasional exaggerations, on the grounds that the cause to which he is committed (the 'cause of Jesus') is a well-intentioned one.

There is no part of the faith (from the existence of God to the truth of final consummation) and of Christian morality, which is not affected and, directly or indirectly, damaged by the craze for change of Küng's anarchical humanism.[133] But all these individual deformations and changes of meaning he introduces are derived from one basic defect: his complete failure to understand the mystery which forms the horizon of the Christian faith – in which alone the truths of Christianity preserve their depth and their supernatural dimension. This horizon he sweeps away, so that the details also become shapeless and disappear. For example, he says that God is not 'an enigmatic God' (Chr 446), that he is 'not in himself, but for mankind and world' and is in strict 'correlation' (that is, mutual relationship, complementariness) to the world, so that in the work of the world he gains something (DG 649). The Trinity is 'not an impenetrable mystery' (Chr 476), but 'the one action of God himself' in his meeting with mankind (DG 701). A man approaches this God through an unprovable and unproved 'basic confidence in reality' (DG 571) which even an atheist can have (DG 571). The pre-existence of Christ is a code word to indicate that what happened in Jesus 'is explained in its first source . . . in the light of the eternal God alone' (DG 685). The earthly birth of Christ is therefore no mystery (DG 685, 689): Joseph is the real father of Jesus (Chr 149,

80

167); Mary is not the Mother of God, 'since God cannot be born' (Chr 460); the death of Christ is a 'call to renounce a life of selfishness' (DG 689); resurrection means that Jesus 'died into' the ultimate reality of God (DG 679): but this (for Jesus as well as for us) is 'going into reality, not going out' (DG 678). For this reason, he rejects the use of the expression 'vision of God' to describe the eternal life of the faithful (DG 522).

Since all these facts and truths which make up the history of salvation are distorted or entirely emptied of meaning, one can see how Küng arrives at his summary of the meaning of Christian faith: 'Christology or Christ theory may be important, but belief in Christ and the following of Christ are more important' (DG 688). But what does this following of Christ, which is finally offered as the decisive criterion, look like? It does not at all mean an interior assimilation to Christ, a spiritual, interior union with him in the sense of St Paul's 'Christ lives in me' (Gal 2:20). The 'living Christ does not call for ineffective adoration, still less to mystic union' (DG 692). It is more a matter of the development of a 'model of being human . . . which enables me to discover and realize the meaning of my being human and of my freedom, in existing and involving myself for my fellow men' (DG 688). Christianity and the following of Jesus mean here putting a humanitarian programme into action.

The radical humanity to be attained in the 'following of Christ' is after all not such a tall order. This is shown by Küng's remarkable criticism of the devotion of Christians to the cross, which basically withdraws all he previously said about the commitment of human existence to the cross. Precisely under the heading 'Following the cross' one would have expected that what is specifically Christian would appear here at last — for example, in a reference, even a restrained one, to the ultimate Christian witness and to martyrdom as the highest and most distinctive expression of a 'Christian humanism'. But, significantly, at this very point, Küng launches into an attack on a Catholic bishop from Eastern Europe who dared to refer to present-day tendencies towards 'an emptying of the Cross' (cf. 1 Cor 1:17). The bishop, who certainly must have had many experiences of the cross in a world hostile to Christ, is reproached for using the cross as a 'sledge hammer' (Chr 573). (Here too the very turn of phrase should be noticed.) The only following of the cross that he seems to allow is that of the 'understood cross' (Chr 576). That is precisely 'not a literal re-enactment of his [Christ's] cross' but a simple enduring of suffering or, better still, not only 'fighting, but utilizing suffering' (Chr 578). The biblical idea of 'being glad to suffer insult for the name of Jesus' (Act 5:41) or the Pauline 'I fill up what is wanting in the sufferings of Christ' are far away from thinking of this type.

I don't mean that Küng's ideas about the imitation of Christ, the cross, and suffering are valueless and have no relevance. I grant that they are 'humanistic' and perhaps even 'radically humanistic'. But they are not as a result specifically Christian: they are once more mere derivatives of a purely natural *theologia crucis*, as different from the supernatural mystery of the cross, as a philosophical statement differs from a confession of faith. Even in evaluating suffering and cross, which Küng considers to be decisive in radical Christian humanism, he does not succeed in indicating what is specifically Christian about his approach. Christianity is certainly something more than 'radical humanism'.

This 'more' is shown in an idea handed down by tradition, and used in the liturgy, which meets with the sharpest and almost cynical rejection from Küng. I refer to the statement firmly contained in explicit Christian faith that 'God has become man, so that man might become God'. Küng challenges this statement (challenged in similar terms, without any evidence, by the agnostic E. Topitsch)[134] by asking: 'Does any sensible person today still want to become God?' True, this statement, which is part of genuine Christian tradition, must not be interpreted in the sense of some pantheistic doctrine of divinisation. But the correct understanding of it, which the ordinary faithful can be thoroughly trusted to have, brings out the precise difference between the Christian and the 'radically humanistic' interpretations of reality and the world process. The Christian does believe that 'man rises infinitely above his human nature' (Pascal) and that this upward movement will one day reach its goal – a share in the inner life of the Trinity. This sharing is already prepared in advance by the sacraments, and does not depend on any Christian social work in the world (which, for example, is just not possible for those Christians who suffer persecution under marxist atheism). For this book the ultimate objective of Christianity is the 'humanisation of man' (Chr 443). This 'Christian' programme can be reduced to one sentence (and its inadequacy thereby easily exposed): a Christianity (*Christlichkeit*) which is saddled with an ideology is concerned to prove that all reality (including the divine reality, which is not clearly distinguished here from the human) exists for the sake of mankind. For genuine Christianity that is only half the truth. For it this is the whole truth: 'All is yours, but you are Christ's, but Christ is God's' (1 Cor 3:23). To put it another way: for radical humanism the good of mankind is the ultimate objective; for the Christian it is the glory of God, in which the good of mankind is also included. But Küng's theology expressly denies that God intends glory or wishes it. Thus again the Christian mystery of God and the world is robbed of its intrinsic significance.

This so-called following of Christ really means getting nowhere fast. This becomes clear in its idea of ethics, which naturally also falls victim to

Küng's radical course correction. Where the teaching and truth of Christianity have been buried, they must, as it were, be resurrected ethically and morally. This accounts for the moralising sections of these books, which in part are penetrating (Chr 530-553; DG 465-473, 578-583).

The peculiarity, and intrinsic illogicality, of this new 'autonomous ethic' are already clear from Küng's basic declaration that there is no such thing as a specifically Christian ethic. His ideas on masturbation and homosexuality (DG 117) and on premarital sexual intercourse and abortion make this quite clear.[135] The consideration in the New Testament of some particular ethical requirement does not mean that this is specifically Christian and as such without parallel (Chr 543). This ethic should not have any significance 'since Jesus is the only significance' (quoted from Bonhoeffer: Chr 541). When, however, this content is scrutinised in more detail, one realises that Küng emphasises only 'what modern man wants to see in Jesus. . . . That emphasis is put on the goodness, philanthropy, sympathetic condescension, anti-hierarchical and anti-institutional attitude of the Lord.'[136] But even these attitudes (in no way specifically Christian) are subject to man's freedom of conscience and (in the moment of decision) to the situation as constituting the sole source of obligation. All these 'attitudes' (one cannot speak of absolute norms) are valid only when a person wants them to be valid. This is confirmed by the statement that 'the good, the moral, is not simply what is abstractly good or correct but what is concretely good or correct for this man or this group: [it is] what is appropriate' (DG 582); under these circumstances obligation can become absolute in the situation, but only on account of the situation and man's subjective judgment. What this means is that there is no such thing as unconditional obligation. Here the essential character of morality is misunderstood. Morality does not consist in a person directing his actions according to a transitory and subjective norm, but instead in the unconditional nature of moral value and of the divine command which comes to man with absolute validity in interhuman relations as well (though Küng disagrees: DG 582). H. Kuhn rightly points to a resemblance here to the sophist, Protagoras, who makes 'man to be the criterion of morality'[137], in spite of all Küng has previously said about the reality of God as the condition of human moral autonomy (DG 579). Thus a reviewer of a lecture by Küng: 'Most contributors to the discussion obviously have difficulty in seeing why you need to bring God into this doctrine which is entirely based on the individual man's freedom and self-fulfilment.'[138] Küng's 'autonomous ethic' should take its own claim seriously and renounce the hypothesis of 'God'. It cannot appeal to Kant: as M. Baumgartner showed in the course of the discussion, Kant conceived moral autonomy as something quite independent of the existence of God.[139]

In what direction, therefore, is this new course pointing, which Küng wishes to give to the Christian faith? Firstly, in no way does it point to the future, as he keeps claiming: his decisive positions, whether in doctrine about God, or in Christology or in ethics, are only a resumption of long-known and dead errors which Küng can foist as new only on to an uninformed public. To this extent you could say his whole intellectual journey is 'a progress into a religiously backward society'.[140] He keeps claiming that he is giving new orientations in an age without orientation: but all he gives is loose thinking, indistinct phraseology – not the truth. He accuses all who don't share his views of being 'under educated' (DG 117), but it is himself who deserves this reproach.

The course he follows in these books is no longer directed by the valid and permanent fixed stars of supernatural revelation, tradition, and the community of faith which is the Church, but by nothing other than a humanism confined to the world. Honest humanists will only ask themselves: Why should this sort of thinking be described as Christian?

The truth is that the Christianity Küng offers has lost its alignment with the transcendent, with mystery, with the supernatural and thus with the Christian stumbling-block (of the cross). Seen in this way, this ship is not at all keeping course towards a higher supernatural goal, but is moving around in a circle of conventional bourgeois humanism. By restricting God to the world and withdrawing divinity from Jesus Christ, it allows itself to be driven by the waves of the spirit of the age, which merges Christianity and the figure of Jesus Christ in the general history of mankind and reduces both to a consumer good of religious sociology and psychology.

The Church, which possesses and must protect the fullness of Christ, cannot be satisfied with such a substitute for faith in Christ, no matter how superficially attractive. Another way will have to be followed, a way which is hard but entirely full of hope, if the Church is to pass on to mankind, without any diminution, the entire 'breadth and the length, the height and the depth of the mystery of Christ' (Eph 3:18). In doing this, the Church may be confident that genuine, original Christianity, proclaimed with living faith and awareness of the true needs of mankind, will ultimately be more convincing and more attractive than home-made imitations, arbitrary compromises and ephemeral striving for effect.

STATEMENT BY THE CONGREGATION FOR THE DOCTRINE OF THE FAITH ON SOME KEY POINTS OF THE THEOLOGICAL TEACHING OF PROFESSOR KÜNG

The Church of Christ has received from God the mandate to keep and to safeguard the deposit of faith so that all the faithful, under the guidance of the magisterium through which Christ himself exercises his role as teacher in the Church, may hold without fail to the faith once delivered to the saints, may penetrate it more deeply by accurate insights, and may apply it more thoroughly to life.[1]

In order to fulfil the important task entrusted to itself alone[2] the magisterium of the Church avails itself of the work of theologians, especially those who in the Church have received from the authorities the task of teaching and who therefore have been designated in a certain manner as teachers of the truth. Theologians, like scholars in other scientific fields, enjoy a legitimate liberty in their research, though within the limits of the method of theology. Thus, while working in their own way, they seek to attain the same specific end as the magisterium itself, namely, 'to preserve, to penetrate even more deeply, to explain, to teach, to defend the sacred deposit of revelation; and in this way to illuminate the life of the Church and of the human race with the light of divine truth.'[3]

It is necessary therefore, that, in theological research and teaching of Catholic doctrine, fidelity to the magisterium should be clearly visible, since no one may rightly act as a theologian except in close union with the mission of teaching truth which is incumbent on the magisterium.[4] When such fidelity is absent harm is done to all the faithful who, since they are bound to profess the faith which they have received from God through the Church, have a sacred right to receive the word of God uncontaminated; therefore they rightly expect vigilant care to be exercised to keep the threat of error far from them.[5]

If it should happen, therefore, that a teacher of theology chooses and disseminates as the norm of truth his own judgment and not the interpretation of the faith given by the Church, and if he continues in his attitude despite the use of all charitable means in this regard, then honesty itself demands that the Church should publicly call attention to his conduct and should decide that he can no longer teach with the authority of the mission which he received from her.[6]

This canonical mission is in fact a testimony to a reciprocal trust: first, trust on the part of the competent authority in a theologian who conducts himself as a Catholic theologian in the work of his research and teaching; secondly, trust on the part of the theologian himself in the Church and in her integral teaching, since it is by her mandate that he carries out his task.

Since some of the writings (spread throughout many countries) and the teaching of Professor Hans Küng, a priest, are a cause of confusion in the minds of the faithful, the Bishops of Germany and this Congregation for the Doctrine of the Faith, acting in common accord, have several times counselled and warned him, wishing to persuade him to carry on his theological work in full communion with the authentic magisterium of the Church.

In this spirit the Sacred Congregation for the Doctrine of the Faith, to fulfil its role of promoting and safeguarding the doctrines of faith and morals in the universal Church[7], issued a public document on 15 February 1975, declaring that some opinions of Professor Hans Küng were opposed in different degrees to the doctrine of the Church which must be held by all the faithful. Among these opinions it noted especially, as of greater importance, those which pertain to the dogma of faith about infallibility in the Church, and to the duty of authentically interpreting the unique sacred deposit of the word of God which has been entrusted only to the living magisterium of the Church, and finally to his views about the valid consecration of the Eucharist.

At the same time this Sacred Congregation warned Professor Küng that he should not continue to teach such opinions, expecting in the meantime that he would bring his opinions into harmony with the doctrines of the authentic magisterium.[8]

However, up to the present time Professor Küng has in no way changed his opinion on the matters called to his attention.

This fact is particularly evident in connectiom with his opinion which at least expresses doubt about the dogma of infallibility in the Church or reduces it to some kind of basic indefectibility of the Church in the truth, while admitting the possibility of error in doctrinal statements which the magisterium of the Church teaches must be held definitely. On this point Hans Küng has in no way sought to harmonise his interpretation with the doctrine of the magisterium. Instead he has recently proposed his view again even more explicitly (particularly in *Kirche-Gehalten in der Wahrheit?*: Benzinger Verlag, 1979 and 'Zum Geleit', an introduction to the work of A.B. Hasler entitled *Wie der Papst unfehlbar wurde*: Piper Verlag, 1979), even though this Sacred Congregation had affirmed that such an opinion contradicts the doctrine defined by Vatican I and confirmed by Vatican II.

Moreover, the logical consequences of this opinion, especially a contempt for the magisterium of the Church, are found in other works published by him, with serious harm to some essential points of Catholic faith (e.g. those teachings which pertain to the consubstantiality of Christ with his Father, and to the Blessed Virgin Mary): truths have been given an interpretation different from the Church's understanding of them in the past and in the present.

The Sacred Congregation for the Doctrine of the Faith in the aforesaid document of 1975 refrained at the time from further action regarding the above-mentioned opinions of Professor Küng, presuming that he himself would abandon them. But since this presumption no longer exists, this Congregation by reason of its duty finds itself constrained to declare that Professor Hans Küng has departed in his writings from the integral truth of Catholic faith, and therefore he can no longer be considered a Catholic theologian nor function as such in a teaching role.

At an audience granted to the undersigned Cardinal Prefect, on 15 December 1949, the Supreme Pontiff Pope John Paul II approved this Declaration, decided upon at an ordinary meeting of this Sacred Congregation, and ordered its publication.

In Rome, at the Sacred Congregation for the Doctrine of the Faith, on 15 December 1979.

(Signed) Franjo Cardinal Seper, *Prefect*

(Signed) Fr Jerome Hamer, OP, Titular Archbishop of Lorium, *Secretary*

1. Cf. Conc. Vatic. I, Const. dogm. *Dei Filius*, cap. IV 'De fide et ratione': DS 3018; Conc. Vatic. II, Const. dogm. *Lumen Gentium* 12.   2. Cf. Conc. Vatic. II, Const. dogm. *Dei Verbum* 10.   3. Paul VI, *Allocut. ad Congress. Internat. de Theologia Conc. Vatic. II,* 1 October 1966; *AAS* 58 (1966), p. 891.   4. Cf. John Paul II, Const. apost. *Sapientia Christiana,* art. 70; Encycl. *Redemptor Hominis* 19; *AAS* 71 (1979) pp. 493, 308.   5. Cf. Conc. Vatic. II, Const. dogm. *Lumen Gentium* 25; Paul VI Adhort. apost. *Quinque iam anni: AAS* 63 (1971) p. 99f.   6. Cf. *Sapientia Christiana,* tit. III, art. 27, par. 1: *AAS* 71 (1979), p. 483.   7. Cf. Motu proprio *Integrae Servandae,* n. 1, 3 and 4: *AAS* 57 (1965) p. 954.   8. Cf. *AAS* 67 (1975) pp. 303-304.

THE GERMAN BISHOPS
AND THE KÜNG AFFAIR

On 7 January 1980 the German Bishops published the following Statement (to be read in all churches in the country) on the measures taken by the Congregation for the Doctrine of the Faith with regard to Professor Küng. With the Statement went a more detailed Explanation. Both these texts are reproduced below. The Explanation, in turn, refers to a published Dokumentation, *consisting of the main documents dealing with the whole affair.*

STATEMENT

In the discussion with Professor Hans Küng, the Pope and the Bishops had an important decision to make. It was necessary to withdraw from him his authority to teach theology in the name of the Church. To many people who were seeking and questioning, Professor Küng opened up ways of approaching fundamental religious problems, but certain concepts he formulated also caused confusion in many believers.

We, the German Bishops, in spite of attempts at clarifications and dialogue that lasted for years, find ourselves, unfortunately, obliged to declare, in full unity with the Pope, that on important points of faith Professor Küng defends opinions that are in conflict with the binding doctrine of the Church. As long as this is the case, he cannot be a teacher of theology in the name of the Church. We make no judgment about Professor Küng's personal beliefs, but about what he writes and what he says in his lectures.

In the last few weeks a great many different things have been said about the Küng case. Were the steps taken against him just? Do not the points in question concern marginal problems? Is the Church returning to the period preceding the Second Vatican Council? How does the matter of freedom in the Church stand? We bishops owe the faithful and public opinion a word of clarification and help. This short statement can of course touch only on some points. We have set forth the details in an exhaustive explanation.

1. In the foreground of the discussions is the word 'infallible'. That no one in the Church, not even the pope, is exempt from error and faults in what he says and does, is obvious. But the doctrine of infallibility in the Church does not concern this. It affirms rather that when the pope, as the supreme teacher of the Church, or an ecumenical Council, or the bishops

88

unanimously with the pope, declare something to be revealed by God and propose it as an article of faith, then the assistance of the Holy Spirit preserves them from error (cf. *Lumen Gentium* 25). Professor Küng, however, questions this. Yet it is clear to him how much the problem of infallibility in the Church concerns the foundations of the faith, Church and theology.

2. Professor Küng has stressed repeatedly that he does not want to contest the binding doctrine of theChurch but only ask it 'questions'. But there is a considerable difference between asking what an affirmation means and how it is justified, and questioning the very affirmation itself and thus doubting it. Professor Küng clearly casts doubt on the binding doctrine of the Church.

3. Is infallibility in the Church not a marginal problem? For faith and theology it is decisive that each one should know on what he must and can base the obedience of faith due to God. Therefore it is not at all a secondary matter if God has promised to the magisterium of the pope and of the bishops that assistance which excludes error in the fundamental articles of faith, thus giving us that certainty in faith on which our life and our hope are based. Of course, all human affirmations, even those of revelation and of the Church, are limited. But limitation and error are different things.

4. If we cannot rely with absolute certainty on the dogmatic affirmations of the Church, then it may even be doubted who Jesus Christ is. Did God really offer himself for us, in that his eternal Son, consubstantial with him, assumed our humanity and died for us? This is the faith that sustains our life and death. It was proclaimed definitively by the great councils of Christian antiquity: for them it represented the central message of the New Testament. Their declarations are and remain for us Christians the foundation of our whole faith and life. We make them ours in the Creed at Holy Mass: 'God from God, Light from Light, true God from true God, begotten, not made, of one Being with the Father.' The affirmations of Professor Küng — in spite of all the attempts of the Congregation, which was concerned to arrive, in dialogue with him, at an unequivocal clarification — fall short of what Holy Scripture, the Creed, the councils and liturgy testify about Jesus Christ.

5. The question is asked again and again whether the procedure against Professor Küng was just. We willingly admit that the procedural systems in the Church can be improved. Yet we must answer clearly that the procedure was just. What is not just is to regard the matter involved in the discussion with Professor Küng as secondary to the question of procedure.

There has been widespread discussion in the media about Professor Küng's opinions on the doctrine about Jesus Christ and on infallibility in the Church. A large number of his fellow theologians have taken up a critical position with regard to his affirmations.

Many letters, talks, invitations to dialogue on the part of the Holy See and of the bishops could not bring Professor Küng to make the necessary contribution to the clarification of the points in discussion. Because Professor Küng let it be known that he was ready to revise his statements, the Congregation for the Doctrine of the Faith, on 15 February 1975, did not insist on their withdrawal and merely exhorted him not to repeat those concepts which were not in agreement with the magisterium of the Church. Professor Küng did not obey. In a publication of 1979 he interpreted the fact that the Church had not withdrawn his authorization to teach as a sign that the magisterium of the Church itself was not sure of its position in the matter of infallibility. Therefore the Pope and the bishops felt obliged to act. They had no alternative but to declare that as long as Professor Küng contradicts the binding doctrine of the Church, he may not teach theology in the name of the Church.

To speak here of violation of human rights or of inquisitorial methods, is not in conformity with the facts. Anyone who examines the documentation of the German Episcopal Conference on the Küng case and also the efforts in the last few weeks, will be convinced that the Congregation was genuinely ready to discuss the matter. It is all the more regrettable that the matter should have had to end with the withdrawal of Professor Küng's ecclesiastical authorization to teach. But we all, together with the Holy Father, still hope that Professor Küng will revise his attitude and his opinions.

In conclusion, we would like to point out expressly that the Church needs theological science and theologians. The basis of theology is the binding faith of the Church. But this faith must be understood, explained and proved in a theological way. This task of theology is of vital importance for the Church. Thus the dialogue between the ministry of the Church and theology is indispensable. We will continue undeterred to seek it.

We, the German Bishops, confirm our full unity with the Holy Father and among ourselves. The worship of the Son of God become man, the profession of faith in him in conformity with the Creed of the Church, the 'yes' to the gift of the Spirit who preserves his Church from error in faith, unite us and all the faithful. Let us defend this unity, let us pray for this unity.

Würzburg, 7 January 1980
Signed by all the Bishops of the German Episcopal Conference

EXPLANATION

The decision of the Church to deprive Professor Hans Küng of the ecclesiastical authorization to teach, has caused a sensation inside and outside the Church. We have received many wirtten communications that expressed concern but also many that expressed approval. Immediately after the Christmas period we met at a special session in order to address to you all a joing message of clarification and guidance, approved unanimously.

1. A matter that had been going on for nearly ten years

Since, in spite of the considerable amount of information made available to the media of social communication, the origin of the conflict is not known everywhere to the same extent, a brief presentation is necessary of the main stages of the discussion which took place. The German Episcopal Conference has published the principal facts in an ample *Dokumentation* [the documents of which are referred to here as 'Document 1' etc.], to enable the public to form an impartial picture of the many efforts made.

Already in May 1968 Professor Küng was invited by the Sacred Congregation for the Doctrine of the Faith to a conversation about his book *The Church* [Document 1] The meeting did not take place and Professor Küng did not even send the written explanation that had been requested about the content of the work. In July 1971 a doctrinal enquiry was begun with regard to the book *Infallible?*; at the same time a list of objections and difficulties was sent to him with the request for an answer [Document 2]. When two years later, in spite of renewed invitations, there had been no conversation on the matter, the Sacred Congregation for the Doctrine of the Faith published the doctrinal statement *Mysterium Ecclesiae* which, without giving names and without threatening sanctions, was intended to clarify positively the truths of faith in question. But when the conversation offered to Professor Küng after the publication of this document [Document 3] could not be achieved in the following two years, the Sacred Congregation for the Doctrine of the Faith, on the orders of Pope Paul VI, decided, on 15 February 1975 [Document 4], on an unusual step: it exhorted the theologian 'not to continue to sustain those doctrinal opinions', and desisted for the time being from further action, that is, it suspended the proceedings in the meantime. Professor Küng had opened the way for this when in September 1974 [Document 5] he informed the Congregation for the Doctrine of the Faith that, with a 'period of time for reflection', he did not exclude the possibility that in the course of time he might be able to 'harmonise' his doctrinal ideas with those of the magisterium. This unprecedented solution was unilaterally rendered ineffective by Professor Küng at the beginning of 1979, when he presented his previous theses about infallibility in the Church in an even more extreme form [Document 6]. Independently of the proceedings of the Sacred Congregation for the Doctrine of the Faith, the German Episcopal Conference had sought in vain, from 1976 to 1977, a further clarification of Professor Küng's doctrine on Jesus Christ [Document 7]. Since

91

1970, moreover, there were repeated public calls to action by Küng against the established practice of the Church (regulation of mixed marriages, recognition of ministries, eucharistic communion, ecclesiastical celibacy, ordination of women for the priestly ministry, etc.) [Cf. Document 8].

In spite of pressing invitations no conversation with Rome took place. The talks with the German Episcopal Conference did not bring a sufficient clarification. Even a long theological discussion failed to induce Professor Küng to make completions which he himself had recognized as being necessary, or even corrections. All the means available to reach a clarification by means of dialogue were used by the Congregation for the Doctrine of the Faith and the German Episcopal Conference. The Holy Father suspended with an extraordinary measure the implementation of the 'Statement' of the Congregation, to allow for further examination. Just a day before the conversation of a delegation of German bishops with Pope John Paul II, which took place on 28 December 1979, Küng through a collaborator, bluntly rejected the urgent request of the Bishop of Rottenburg-Stuttgart, territorially competent, for some clarifications regarding content [Document 9]. With that the decision to implement the Statement became inevitable.

2. Objective reasons for the decision of the Church

In the discussions that have arisen since the notification of the decision on 18 December 1979, the events themselves have been placed in the foreground, while the substantial problems have been in danger of disappearing from view. What exactly is the matter at issue?

a) It is a question not only of the infallibility of the pope but of the whole Church, and even of the truth of Holy Scripture. Professor Küng recognizes that the Church of Jesus Christ is promised a fundamental permanence in God's truth. Nearly all Christian churches and ecclesial communities affirm in their declarations of faith this permanence of the Church in the unfailing faithfulness of God. He gave himself to the world in Jesus Christ once and for all, and he entrusted the word of salvation to his Church to be preserved faithfully and transmitted exactly in the course of time. This permanence of the Church in the truth promised by God does not exclude, however, individual errors. Professor Küng believes that a global remaining in truth is sufficient. Yes – and this is the core of his thesis – this is compatible with concrete errors in definitions of faith that the magisterium of the Church has promulgated as irrevocable. Thus Professor Küng denies that 'the permanence of the Church in truth is bound up with definite dogmas or authorities'. Thereby he questions not only the infallibility of the pope, but antecendently and far more fundamentally the gift operated by the Spirit to preserve the Church in the truth of God. Defence from error by means of an active protection of the treasures of faith and, even more so, a definitive decision in problems of faith would no longer be possible.

b) With this fundamental thesis, Professor Küng obscures two other dimensions of Christian faith. These are the definitive nature of the Creed, and a certainty which persists through life and death. Therefore the Creed, expressed in absolute terms, has been closely linked from the beginning with biblical faith. Only in this way, through the certainty of faith, can the Christian have joy and confidence even in difficult situations. Non-Catholic Christian churches and ecclesial communities are also convinced of this. Professor Küng does not deny the need to express the faith by means of formulas. But he questions the permanent validity of absolutely binding definitions. Obviously the Church does not deny that these formulas of faith, marked by earlier ways of thought, can and must be more deeply understood and explained pastorally in a new way.

A second difficulty is closely connected with these fundamental theses: for Professor Küng it is no longer clear that the Church in its official authorities (episcopal college, council, pope), faced with a determined historical situation, has the power of expressing infallibly in dogmatic terms the profession of Christian faith (cf. dogmatic Constitution on the Church of the Second Vatican Council, *Lumen Gentium* 25).

In these situations the competent ministers do not exercise power in an arbitrary way but are official and public witnesses to the purity of the living heritage of faith. They are the mouth-piece of the witness of faith of the whole Church. Their public function in the Church is therefore geared to the proclamation of faith. 'This Magisterium is not superior to the Word of God, but is its servant' (Dogmatic Constitution on divine revelation, Second Vatican Council, 10). The Church has always been convinced that for the responsible implementation of the specific service of witness, she is granted special assistance from the Holy Spirit. There can be no question of arbitrary and self-complacent exercise of power by the magisterium of the Church.

c) These elements of the understanding of faith are summed up in the concept of infallibility in the Church. It certainly does not hold the same central position in the faith as the question of God and the resurrection of Christ, but it is far from being a 'marginal dogma'. It helps to find truth and to inspire confidence in official teaching and in this way is indirectly of benefit to members of the Church. The faithful are entitled to a complete and clear exposition of the inalienable truths of faith. And therefore a theologian's position with regard to ultimate and binding affirmations of faith makes it possible to discern how he understands revelation and history, the Spirit and the Church, the ministry and the word. When something goes wrong in this field, there appear dangerous cracks, even if at first they are hardly perceptible, in the foundation of his theology and also in the conviction of faith of the community. We German Bishops, in a detailed declaration of 17 February 1975, had already drawn attention to these consequences of Professor Küng's theological method. This, too, was in vain.

d) These defects are evident above all in Professor Küng's affirmations about the person of Jesus Christ. He would like, certainly, to abide by 'the great intentions and contents of the ecumenical Councils', but his concrete affirmations on the divinity of Jesus Christ and on the Holy Trinity fall short of the content of the faith handed down. For example, it is not wrong, but it is not sufficient, to say 'that in the history of Jesus Christ God and man are really at work'. For the Christian faith it is decisive to profess that Jesus Christ is absolutely and from all eternity the Word of God. 'We believe ... in Jesus Christ Our Lord, the Only Son of God, born of the Father before all time; God from God, Light from Light, true God from true God, begotten, not made, of one Being with the Father'.

The attempt must certainly be made to explain these words of the Great Creed to modern men. But the theologian must never be vague on this decisive point of the Christian creed. It is a question, in fact, of the truth of our salvation: if in Jesus Christ it was not God himself who gave himself to men, then Jesus Christ cannot redeem us from sin and death. On this point all Christian Churches are agreed. All affirmations about the humanity of Jesus and his human exemplarity are significant for believers only if they are closely connected with the absolute affirmation of 'true God'. The Roman Statement does not formally present the Christological problem as the fundamental reason for the withdrawal of Professor Küng's authorization to teach. This reason is due to juridical and procedural causes because the doctrinal discussion, which has been going on for nearly ten years, did not initially include this problem. The fact that mention of the Christological problem is made incidentally does not mean that this and other inaccuracies (e.g. with regard to the Mother of God and the Sacraments) should be taken less seriously. The German Episcopal Conference referred to their essential significance exhaustively in its message on the book *On being a Christian* published on 17 November 1977 addressed to preachers of the faith. These references are important precisely from the ecumenical point of view.

3. Settlement and consequence

After the failure of all attempts to reach a clarification, a decision had become unavoidable, particularly owing to the importance of the problems. All those responsible for this decision were painfully aware of its pastoral significance. Küng's theological work was not all to be rejected, but only the above-mentioned points. The pastoral purpose of his work has always been recognized by us. It is not a question of a global rejection of his theology. But it was becoming a more and more unbearable contradiction in the Church that a theologian of great influence, teaching on behalf of the Church, and forming future theologians, priests and laity, should act for years contrary to the office he had received. It is a question of transmitting the treasures of Catholic faith intact to other generations and not of a claim to power on the part of Rome or the self-preservation of a system.

We understand the concern of many people. We ask, however, for confidence when we declare with Pope John Paul II that in the relationship between the magisterium and theology we want to preserve the spirit of mutual understanding and dialogue. No one can and wants to fall short of the letter and spirit of the Second Vatican Council. We are not afraid and we are not closed with regard to the inevitable problems and researches of theology. On the contrary: from the most remote past difficulties between theology and ministry of the Church — often unnoticed by public opinion — have been solved in a conciliatory way. We beg you to consider the case of Professor Küng as a very concrete exception which we tried to settle amicably for nearly ten years. In no case shall we abandon this style in the future. Nor do the Pope and the Congregation wish to do so. But neither can we fail in our duty of preserving the faith, for the fulfilment of which we will be answerable to the judgment of God. On taking up his office, the theologian has been entrusted with teaching the living faith of the Church. There remains a wide field for his own questions and new research. He must not forget, however, that he is working for the building up of the Church. He cannot of himself alone judge whether he is successful in doing so. If he unilaterally betrays the confidence placed in him, if he sets himself up as his own yardstick, and if as a result his teaching authorization has to be withdrawn, it is deceitful and dishonest to speak of violation of human rights. Professor Küng's freedom of opinion is not limited in any way.

An appeal has often been made to the ecumenical dimension of the conflict. But it is not a question exclusively, or even primarily, of special Catholic doctrines. On the contrary, the irrevocable truth of the Bible and of the decisions of the ancient councils of the Church, is really fundamental. By taking up a position in favour of the complete profession of faith in Christ, we think we are rather doing a service to the whole of Christendom.

We do not wish to retreat from positions already reached, but neither do we wish to take irresponsible steps, which actually do not mean progress. All of us will draw closer to one another if we become more similar to Jesus Christ. To do so, we must change. To surrender a doctrine which is also held by one's partner, is no help in the search for unity. We thank many Protestant sisters and brothers for their discreet concern when a family conflict is being settled in their neighbour's house. They themselves know only too well that our questions and difficulties are also — perhaps in a different form — their problems. They, too, are obliged at times to carry out disciplinary procedures in doctrinal matters.

We thank theologians for their laborious and disinterested work. We ask them to be patient and prudent when making their hypotheses public. It is much better that they should themselves criticise and correct the orientation of their work than that they should be the subject of an ecclesiastical enquiry.

We ask all members of our church and all those interested in the matter to judge dispassionately the decision that has been taken. It is not possible to call for love without at the same time caring about truth. Tolerance does not mean renunciation of the search for truth. Pluralism in theology is not possible without the necessary unity of faith. Do not trust slogans and propaganda which may, in the long run, jeopardize the peace and unity of the Church.

We are aware of our special responsibility to the universal Church, in close union with Pope John Paul II, the Bishop of Rottenburg-Stuttgart and all the faithful of that diocese. In conclusion we ask you for your prayer, so that God will preserve his Church from harm and from discord.

Würzburg, 7 January 1980
Signed by all the members of the German Episcopal Conference

NOTES

1. Cf. K. Rahner, 'Opposition in der Kirche' in *Schriften zur Theologie* XII (Einsiedeln 1975), p. 476   2. *Aufstand der Massen* [*The Revolt of the Masses*] (Gesammelte Werke III) (Stuttgart 1978), pp. 84ff; 110   3. K. Lehmann (and others), *Theologie der Befreiung* (Einsiedeln 1977), p. 16   4. *Existiert Gott? Antwort auf die Gottesfrage der Neuzeit* (Munich 1978), p. 213. English version: *Does God exist? An Answer for Today*   5. *Gesam-*

melte Schriften III (Munich 1978), p. 213 * Translated by Edward Quinn (London 1976) from the Munich 1974 edition; references in this book relate to the London 1978 paperback edition. 6. 'Ein Jahr Johannes Paul II' in *Frankfurter Allgemeine Zeitung*, 13 October 1979 7. *Die Einheit in der Kirche* (ed. J.R. Geiselmann, Cologne 1957), p. 107 8. Cf. on this point the summary in L. Scheffczyk, *Aufbruch oder Abbruch des Glaubens* (Stein am Rhein 1976), pp. 7-11. Some passages are here quoted from this essay. Cf. also A. Kolping, *Der 'Fall Küng'* (Bergen-Enkheim 1975). 9. Mainz 1976 10. Ibidem, p. 15 11. Ibidem, p. 16 12. Ibidem, p. 25 13. It was recently rejected by the Evangelical historian of dogma, A. Adam, in *Lehrbuch der Dogmengeschichte* I (Gütersloh 1965), p. 139. 14. *Diskussion*, p. 81 15. Ibidem, p. 62 16. Ibidem, p. 48 17. Ibidem, p. 105 18. Ibidem, p. 90 19. Ibidem, p. 126 20. Ibidem, p. 128 21. Ibidem, p. 121 22. Ibidem, pp. 107f 23. Ibidem, p. 135 24. J. Bökmann, 'Christsein= Menschsein? Zur Banalisierung der Glaubensexistenz' in *Schulinformationen* 7 (1975), pp. 2-11. 25. W. Jens (ed.), *Um nichts als die Wahrheit* (Munich 1978), p. 178. Cited as *Wahrheit*. 26. E. Laws, 'Nein, Herr Professor Küng' in *Ermlandbuch 1977*, pp. 49-84. Later: *Küng un das Glaubensbekenntnis* (St Augustin, nr. Bonn 1978). 27. Ibidem, p. 76 28. Ibidem, p. 81 29. Ibidem, p. 82 30. *Wahrheit*, p. 195 31. *Does God exist?*, p. 23 and 705 32. Cf. letter of the Congregation for the Doctrine of the Faith, 15 February 1975: *Wahrheit*, pp. 142-145. 33. Declaration of the German Bishops Conference after the examination of *Christ sein* and their first statement of their attitude to it, 15 February 1975: *Wahrheit* , pp. 146-151. 34. Ibidem, p. 151 35. 24 September 1975 36. *Wahrheit*, p. 187 37. The Stuttgart Colloquium: ibidem, p. 213-313 38. Ibidem, p. 284 39. Ibidem, p. 244 40. Ibidem, p. 255 41. Ibidem, p. 256 42. Cf. Vatican I: Denzinger-Schönmetzer (DS) 3020 43. *Wahrheit*, p. 291 44. Ibidem, p. 336 45. Ibidem, p. 344 46. Ibidem, p. 347 47. Ibidem, p. 351 48. Ibidem, p. 351 49. Ibidem, p. 373 50. Ibidem, p. 376 51. Ibidem, p. 382 52. Ibidem, p. 384 53. Ibidem, p. 384 54. Ibidem, p. 384 55. Ibidem, p. 383 56. Ibidem, pp. 236, 287, 317, 383 57. 'Neue Phase im Streit um Hans Küng' in *Herderkorrespondenz* 32 (1978), p. 163 58. T. P. O'Mahony in the *Irish Press*, 14 January 1977 59. *Wahrheit*, p. 265 60. *Kirchenbote Osnabrück* 37/38, 10 September 1978 61. 'Zur Gottesfrage der Neuzeit' in *Theologische Revue* 74 (1978), pp. 353 & 358 62. F. Weigand, 'Mehr Freiraum für junge katholische Theologen' in *Stuttgarter Zeitung*, 25 March 1978 63. *Philosophische Hinweise zur sicheren Erkennbarkeit der Existenz Gottes* (Munich 1978), p. 56 64. Ibidem, p. 57 65. 'So werden Ketzer zu Kirchenlehrern' in *Rheinische Merkur* 18, 5 May 1978 66. 'Gottesglaube – rational verantwortet' in *Herderkorrespondenz* 32 (1978), pp. 473ff 67. In *Kirchl. Amtsblatt Osnabrück,* 26 September 1978 68. *Das Elend der Theologie: Kritische Auseinandersetzung mit Hans Küng* (Hamburg 1979), p. 122 69. Ibidem, p. 124 70. Ibidem, p. 42 71. Ibidem, p. 82 72. Ibidem, p. 155 73. *Naturwissenschaftliche und religiöse Wahrheit: Schritte über Grenzen,* 2nd ed., (Munich 1971), p.

344. **74.** Cf. *Münchener Theol. Ztschr.* 29 (1978), p. 286 **75.** Cf. G. Siegmund, *Der Kampf um Gott* (Buxheim 1976), p. 5 **76.** *Der Antichrist*, p. 61 **77.** H. Albert, op. cit., p. 157 **78.** *Der Verkehr des Christen mit Gott*, 7th ed., (Tübingen 1920), p. 64 **79.** M. Hengel, *Der Sohn Gottes* (Tübingen 1975), p. 99 **80.** Ibidem, p. 142 **81.** *Wahrheit*, pp. 198f **82.** K. Jaspers and R. Bultmann, *Die Frage der Entmythologisierung* (Munich 1954), p. 11 **83.** *Schöpfung und Geheimnis* (Hamburg 1970), pp. 157f **84.** Ibidem, p. 149 **85.** *Wahrheit*, p. 253 **86.** Ibidem, p. 270 **87.** *Wahrheit und Methode*, 2nd ed., (Tübingen 1965), p. 377 **88.** *Dei Verbum* 6 **89.** H. Verweyen, art. cit, p. 358 **90.** K. Krenn, art. cit. **91.** H.M. Baumgartner, art. cit., p. 358 **92.** Art. cit., p. 475 **93.** H. Albert, op. cit., p. 141 **94.** *Verbum Dei* 1 **95.** J. Hirschberger and J.B. Deninger (eds.), *Gottesbeweise: Vergängliches – Unvergängliches: Denkender Glaube* (Frankfurt 1966), p. 142 **96.** H. Albert, *op. cit.*, p. 83 **97.** Thus J. Ratzinger, 'Christ sein-Plausibel gemacht' in *Theol. Revue* 71 (1975), p. 355 **98.** *An die Römer* (Tübingen 1973), p. 3 **99.** *Das Johannesevangelium* I (Freiburg 1965), pp. 242f **100.** *Wahrheit*, p. 385 **101.** *Wahrheit*, p. 132 **102.** Ibidem, p. 158 **103.** Ibidem, p. 168 **104.** Ibidem, p. 278 **105.** H. Küng (ed.), *Fehlbar? Eine Bilanz* (Zurich 1973) **106.** Ibidem, p. 253 **107.** Eine Ausführliche Stellungnahme erfolgte in *Münich. Theol. Zt.* 25 (1974), pp. 51-63 **108.** *Wahrheit*, p. 160 **109.** A.B. Hasler, *Wie der Papst unfehlbar wurde. Macht und Ohnmacht eines Dogmas. Mit einem Geleitwort von H. Küng* (Munich 1979), p. xv **110.** Ibidem, p. xv **111.** Statement of 15 December 1975: cf Appendix below **112.** In Hasler, p. xxxvi **113.** Ibidem, p. xiii **114.** Ibidem, pp. xvf **115.** Ibidem, p. xxx **116.** Ibidem, p. xxx **117.** Ibidem, p. xxiv **118.** Ibidem, p. xxvi **119.** Ibidem, p. xxvi **120.** Ibidem, p. xxxi **121.** Cf., for example, W. Brandmüller, 'H. Küng und die Kirchengeschichte' in K. Rahner (ed.), *Zum Problem Unfehlbarkeit* (Freiburg 1971), pp. 117-133 **122.** P. Stuhlmacher, 'Neues Testament und Hermeneutik – Versuch einer Bestandsaufnahme' in *Zt. f. Theologie und Kirche* 68 (1971), p. 148 **123.** In Hasler, op. cit., p. xix **124.** P. Stuhlmacher, 'Thesen zur Methodologie gegenwärtiger Exegese' in *Zt. f. neutestamentliche Wissenschaft* 63 (1972), p. 27 **125.** In Hasler, op. cit. p. xix **126.** Ibidem, p. xxxiii **127.** Cf. O. Semmelroth 'A priori unfehlbare Sätze?' in *Zum Problem Unfehlbarkeit*, pp. 196-215 **128.** Ibidem, pp. 202f **129.** Thus in *Unfehlbar?* (Einsiedeln 1970), p. 120 **130.** *Fehlbar?*, p. 50 **131.** Ibidem, p. 229 **132.** In Hasler, p. xxvi **133.** Thus H. Kuhn, 'Woran man sich halten kann' in *Münich. Theol. Zt* 30. 2 (1979), p. 51 **134.** *Gottwerdung und Revolution* (Munich 1973), p. 38. **135.** Cf. on this point 'Ein Jahr Johannes Paul II' in *Frankfurter Allgemeine Zeitung*, 13 October 1979 **136.** B. Stoeckle, 'Zum Ethos und zur Ethik' in *Diskussion*, p. 135 **137.** Art. cit., p. 32 **138.** 'Freiheit und Selbstverwirklichung – wozu dann noch den lieben Gott?' in *Münchener Merkur,* 14 December 1979 **139.** Art. cit., p. 475 **140.** Cf. L. Bossle, *Vorwärts in die Rückgangsgesellschaft* (Würzburg 1979), pp. 117-121